POETOPIA

THE EAST

Edited by Lisa Adlam

First published in Great Britain in 2015 by:

 Young**Writers**

Remus House
Coltsfoot Drive
Peterborough
PE2 9BF
Telephone: 01733 890066
Website: www.youngwriters.co.uk

Printed and bound in the UK by BookPrintingUK
Website: www.bookprintinguk.com

FOREWORD

Welcome, Reader!

For Young Writers' latest competition, Poetopia, we gave secondary school pupils nationwide the challenge of writing a poem based on the rules of one of 5 factions: Castitas for reflective, honest poetry; Temperantia for angry, assertive poetry; Humilitas for positive, uplifting poetry; Benevolentia for emotional poetry; and Industria for diligent, structured poetry. Poets who wrote a poem outside of these parameters were assigned to Dissimîlis.

We chose poems for publication based on style, expression, imagination and technical skill. The result is this entertaining collection full of diverse and imaginative poetry, which is also a delightful keepsake to look back on in years to come.

Here at Young Writers our aim is to encourage creativity in the next generation and to inspire a love of the written word, so it's great to get such an amazing response, with some absolutely fantastic poems. Once all the books in the series are published we will pick the best poem from each faction to win a prize.

I'd like to congratulate all the young poets in Poetopia - **The East** - I hope this inspires them to continue with their creative writing. And who knows, maybe we'll be seeing their names on the best seller lists in the future...

Jenni Bannister
Editorial Manager

THE FACTIONS

CASTITAS (Kas-ti-tas)

- Write a soul-baring, honest poem
- Tell us what it is like to be you
- Channel your confusion and emotions at being a teenager into verse

TEMPERANTIA (Temper-ran-tee-ah)

- Stand up for someone or something
- Vent your anger through poetry
- Express your frustration about a situation that's out of your control

HUMILITAS (Hu-mil-lih-tahs)

- Write a positive, uplifting poem
- Write an ode to celebrate someone or something that you appreciate
- Write a spiritual poem

BENEVOLENTIA (Ben-e-vol-en-tee-ah)

- Write a love / emotional poem
- Empathise with another's situation or predicament
- Write a praise poem
- Write a poem about your best friend / your friendship

INDUSTRIA (In-dust-ree-ah)

- Write a poem about current affairs
- Use a strict poetic form, such as a sonnet or kyrielle
- Research a poet of your choice and write in a similar style

DISSIMĬLIS (Diss-i-mĭl-is)

- If pupils write a poem that falls outside of the factions' rules, they become Dissimĭlis
- Poems can be on any theme or style

CONTENTS

THE
POEMS

 # Smile

Smile, the sun's still shining,
So stop any whining,
Wipe off your frown,
Become the clown.

Smile, the world hasn't ended,
Therefore you will be mended,
You will be happy,
No need for a nappy.

Smile, you're not alone,
Call a friend on the phone,
Somebody's there for you,
Even if at first they're new.

Smile, life goes down,
Yet comes back up,
No need for sadness,
But real need for gladness.

Esme Nice

Conforming

She's been put into a place that teaches you right from wrong,
Good from bad
Maths from science
A place where you can be different
But not too different, otherwise you will be breaking the rules
A place where angst is forbidden
You shall be *kind*
You shall be *blind*
You shall be *smart*
But you have to have some sort of heart
They will teach you necessary things that you will not use in the outside world
She will not question, she will just say yes
Her voice is taken by the leaders because they do not care about the bleeders
However, this doesn't matter since they are teaching her right from wrong.

Zelia Dias (15)

 # No Freedom At All

Be yourself
But don't be you.
What's that in your ear?
One piercing, two?
Be individual
But don't be different.
No funky hair colours, you'll look like an idiot
It's the school rules
That's the way things go.
We'll tell you off
When the true you shows
'Be yourself' that's what they say.
Then why are they trying to make us look a certain way?

Alanna Rose Boyce (14)
Caister High School, Great Yarmouth

3rd Hound

Your energy seeps in me
I feel your electricity
An embrace so warm
I become a storm.

A beginning of empty heat
Where two rivers meet
A tangle of frustration
And a loss of navigation.

A gentle breeze
That sets me free
Is your body
Passing through me?

But I still feel the pressure
That I can never measure
Until you fill me with your presence
Where there is no more room for depressions.

Go ahead
Light your cigarette
Burn the stick of poison
Like you burn my melancholy emotion.

A red collar against your throat
For those who bear your leash with gloat
Let it be me to take the lead
But that's an excuse as you're all I need.

Beam your smile
Across a mile
As that's how I know
To get back home.

Jo Dan Wong (14)
Caister High School, Great Yarmouth

It Was Just A Mistake

That very day
the leaves that lay
beneath my feet,
I skipped a beat.
As I walked towards the light,
I saw you standing there without a fright.

The moment we touched
it was all too much.
The way you came across
made me feel so lost,
there were no feelings to describe
the pain that was inside.

You hurt me once,
you hurt me twice.
I thought you were different,
well, you just ruined my life.

The moment with you
felt like forever,
I didn't want to leave you,
but it was now or never.

I hope you are happy,
I hope you are proud.
You played me enough,
now things are tough.

Yasmine Georgia Melo (14)
Caister High School, Great Yarmouth

My Worst Best Friend

One minute we're best friends
The next we're not.
You make me choose.
Why would you do that?

Our memories are great.
They are forever in my heart
But so are the bad times.
Why would you do that?

You say how much I mean to you.
That our friendship is the best.
But if I meant that much to you
Why would you do that?

You're mostly there for me
And I'm there for you too.
But why couldn't you be there?
Instead you make me choose.

Choose between the two people I love.
Choose between you and him.
You know how much you both mean to me.
So why make me choose?

Shainaya Jones (14)
Caister High School, Great Yarmouth

 # It's Not Easy Being Ginger

It's not easy being ginger
When others point the finger
Just because of our different hair
This is extreme prejudice
And it is quite frankly, unfair.

Gregor Standerwick (13)
Caister High School, Great Yarmouth

Manchester

Look, when I woke up today
I did not think I'd find a path
That led me astray
Into the city of Manchester.
Where you don't know
If the city is blue
Like an old school boy's bed
Or red
Like the Devil's head.

That makes me angry,
You don't know who to laugh at
Who to call a waste of time
Or who to call a stupid lime.

They're all nothin' here
Too busy drinking beer
And talking utter rubbish.

They've got no fans in Manchester
They're all a little thick
They all think they can get drunk on Fanta
And they all fight with a stick.

Zak Ravenhill (13)
Caister High School, Great Yarmouth

The Forgotten Freddo

The appeasing manner in which our time together was spent.
We will not succumb to the infinite pressure of their opinions.
The filthy pigs profiting from our separation.
It is an enigma, the true problem they have with our love.
I need you!

Jacob Robert William Ferguson (13)
Caister High School, Great Yarmouth

 # Perfection

Perfection,
That's what they say,
It's what we get told to be every day,
We have to say the right thing
And be the right person.

Despite inside, we are all broken,
But no, if we speak our feelings,
We get called weak,
This is what we have to get through
Every week of our lives.

Society says we have to be ourselves,
But we can't do that without judging each other,
We push our bodies to the limit,
Just to be normal for a minute.

Life shouldn't be like this,
Full of loneliness and diss,
It brings tears to my eyes
And darkness to our skies,
That's how it ends. In suicide.

Chloe Barber (13)
Caister High School, Great Yarmouth

 # The Agonising Wait

The wait
Agonising
Draining my energy
Every prolonged minute
Stabbing at my conscience
I need it now. The addiction is noxious.
Give me my
Crunchy Nut.

Max Jordan Burgess (14)
Caister High School, Great Yarmouth

The One

Each day you grow
Each day you go
With anger rise above
With love and care
Help everywhere
I love you my dear love.

We have the strength
We have the power
The best that we can be
You're my one
The one which shone
In the light of day.

But now it's dim
You are so grim
You even laugh on three
Just let me ask you this my dear
What's it like to be me?

Leah Jacobs (13)
Caister High School, Great Yarmouth

I Miss You . . .

I close my eyes and wish
I wish you were still here with me
I wish I could hold you in my arms one more time
Now you're with the angels - and I will never see you again . . .

I miss your warmth
I miss your smile
I miss your positive thoughts
I miss your presence
I just miss you . . .

Caitlin Whittington (14)
Caister High School, Great Yarmouth

Why?

Why do we have to be the way you want?
Why is the world under your control?
Why are we different if we are homosexual?
Why are we normal if we are getting As?
Why am I different if I wear a hoodie?
Why are they 'bad' because they walk the streets?
Why can't she fight for us, because of her gender?

Society can't control all of us!
So what if we're teens and cuss,
We wear hoods and have a big group of friends, thus
We are 'stupid teens' and 'ruining our lives'.
Just stop - we are not your toys!
You can't model us into perfect people!
Let us be our own
And stop making us ask . . .
Why?

Laney Williams (13)
Caister High School, Great Yarmouth

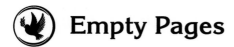

Empty Pages

There are these magical worlds,
Worlds that are explored by many.
The words on the pages,
Appeal to all ages.
The stories and heroes
Will stay in our hearts forever.
We will never forget them.
Never.

The stories never sleep.
Their meanings so deep.
The pen flows across the pages,
As the storm of ideas rages.

Hannah Smith (13)
Caister High School, Great Yarmouth

The Girl

Her pale blue eyes could never change
And if they did, she would look strange.
Her luxurious lips, as red as blood,
They were very different compared to mud.

The clothes she wore could be quite classy,
Even if sometimes she was quite sassy.
The shoes she had on sparkled like the moon,
She was pretty, unlike me, I was a baboon.

I know now, her name is Rose
And I hoped, that as she chose
Her beloved husband, soon to be.
I prayed and I prayed, I hoped it was me.

Sean Yates (14)
Caister High School, Great Yarmouth

Nothing

Rumours go round,
I wish that I knew,
But to find out like this
All I think is, *I hate you.*

The girls always knew
That we'd be cute
'Together forever'
But no, we don't suit.

I cry in the corner
Every day that goes by
But what do you care
You're nothing but sly.

Megan Cork (13)
Caister High School, Great Yarmouth

Perfection

Your hair, your skin, your looks, your size
Down, down, down to your demise
Yet, they push you further every day
Picking on everything you do or say.

Fit in, fit in! Everyone must be the same
Follow the rules of this spiteful game
Have the newest things and look just right
But you will never be 'perfect', try as you might.

Need, need, need material ideas
But fitting in is my greatest fear
I would rather be different than conform to your ways
Tormented and ridiculed for the rest of my days.

Amy Leigh Johnson (13)
Caister High School, Great Yarmouth

The Walking Dead

By far my favourite programme,
The undead roam the streets,
Survivors fighting for their lives,
The viewers on the edge of their seats.

Supplies have run out,
Adding to their despair -
Memories of loved ones forgotten,
Vanished into thin air.

Lost in a world of illness,
Unsure of dangers ahead,
Wanting to be safe and unharmed
Fear the living, fight the dead.

Kyle Le Picq (13)
Caister High School, Great Yarmouth

Society

A once beautiful thing
Turned into such horror.
Satan fighting with Hell
Yet no one understands
Why it's happening.
It's as strong as the wind.
They say it's easy to stop
But it manages to come back.
Always.

Laura Gooch (14)
Caister High School, Great Yarmouth

Dissimilis

You may not like Mondays,
But when you are older you will wish you still had a million,
Life doesn't stop for anyone.
People don't want to rise from their slumbers,
Deep sleeps, whatever you choose to call,
People don't want to learn about the world,
About living,
Think about it, life is amazing,
Get up, live a little, you'll regret it if you don't.

You're all the same, you should be the ones getting judged,
We're individual,
You judge, but all you do is copy,
Each one of you,
Someone's a different, size, religion, so what?
I don't understand you all.
People I know,
Crying, hiding their feelings.
Would you like it if your daughter turned out like you?
Think about that and maybe, just maybe, change!

Chloe Chadwick (12)
Clacton County High School, Clacton-on-Sea

 # Darkness

I share your fears, we all do
That a better day is not to be
And the pain inside how it tortures thee.
That the dark forces that ride will come
And you shall not fight for you feel numb.
That you scream and cry but no one hears your silence
And you live in a world of blackened violence.
That the tears that fall shall not fade
And the walls around you, they shall cascade.
That you're pulled deeper under the water
And ready and lined up for slaughter.
That even though you try
And people can't seem to understand why.
That when it's at your end
And you shall have no friends.
That the tick-tock-tocking of the clock shall never stop
And therefore you shall never be unlocked.
That your final breath is soon to occur
And your life is soon to be a blur.
That your words are never heard
And your thoughts will be slurred.
That all that awaits is black
And when you turn your back,
That all will be gone
And you must go on.

Amber Coppin
Clacton County High School, Clacton-on-Sea

 # Untitled

Bang, bang guns blow
Shots fired here we go
Time to fight, time to win.

Callum Earl (13)
Clacton County High School, Clacton-on-Sea

I Fall

Broken waters flow
In the sea of greed's glow
Fast it is to engulf me
And I'm weightless
A fighter until I'm lifeless.

I fall,
Anger, heat, emotion, rage
I feel these in the infinite blackness
As my heart is ripped
Too fast for me.

I fall,
Suddenly I see red
Anger, over those
Who never saw it.
Especially she.

I fall,
Never to climb
Anger, heat, emotion, rage
I feel a break
And I'm lost, anger consuming me.

I fall,
Now to know
How to feel
It happens again
Rage consumes.

Will I climb?
Will I win?
No, I won't
Never to climb again.

I fall,
Now given in to missing her
Her soul resting
My heart resting
In a pit of fire.

I fall,
Now with blackened will
I try to climb,
I try to win,
But it fails
On a whim.

I give in,
I've hit the bottom,
My heart in ache,
No more light,
No escape.

On the abyss,
I see stars,
To climb again,
Never to fall.

Mark Devine (13)
Clacton County High School, Clacton-on-Sea

 # Happiness

Love is a way to express yourself,
Don't be ashamed about it,
If you are really happy with your best friend,
Just be happy,
Why did you say that?
I understand
You can love your best friend,
I do,
It can sometimes be fun,
It can sometimes be sad,
Just say what you want,
They will understand,
Don't be afraid to say what you feel,
I am yours forever,
Don't cry,
Don't be heartbroken.

Charlie Georgina Chambers (11)
Clacton County High School, Clacton-on-Sea

The Times Of Change

The times of change are upon us,
But, not for the better.
Economics are collapsing
Like the cliffs by the sea.
We can't do anything,
Except revolt.

The times of change are pushing everyone down,
As new rules are made the old disappear.
People protest, 'Bring them back.'
They cry, 'Bring them back!'
Nothing can be done to change minds
Only tanks and death can break bones.

These bring pain,
Pain to us all,
These times of change
We regret placing them
But a new future will be fought.

Riots will come,
The army will come
And bring chaos.
We will remember
The ones who have fallen
In these times of change.

Aaron Morgan
Clacton County High School, Clacton-on-Sea

 **Untitled**

If I work hard
You can too,
Together we can
Be a hard-working crew.

Abbie Ferris (12)
Clacton County High School, Clacton-on-Sea

Life

Always have a smile,
Never a frown.
Always feel like you're wearing a crown.
Love those who love you
And accept those who don't.
Not everyone's perfect
Put their needs before your own.
Be proud of what you have
Some people have nothing.
All of this is true,
I'm really not bluffing.
Everything happens for a reason,
So just trust the future,
Be successful, live your life,
But please don't cause trouble.
Follow your dreams,
Be who you want to be,
Don't let anyone bring you down to your knees.
You were brought into this world for a reason,
So don't end it, be your own person.
Be the one who never stopped smiling,
I promise things will get better
And I promise you I'm not lying.

Chloe Marie Hockton (13)
Clacton County High School, Clacton-on-Sea

Untitled

Aiming at the German people,
Trying to get their temples,
Keeping as quiet as possible,
Living this way soon becomes impossible,
Fighting for survival
Against their biggest rivals.

Jack Wallace Woods (11)
Clacton County High School, Clacton-on-Sea

Tweet! Start! The Whistle Sounds

Tweet! Start!
The whistle sounds,
Running over lush green grass,
My life, for now,
Becomes complete,
With a ball down at my feet,
I glance across the bright green sea
And sail my treasure through the waves,
Passing sharks on my way,
I see an opening . . .
Shoot! Missed.

My boots shudder in the squelchy mud,
My heart pounding with excitement,
My stolen treasure comes into view across the sea,
Tweet! Foul!
Wait . . . wait . . .
The play resumes,
Running again,
This 90-minute joy will never end.

Harry McCarthy (12)
Clacton County High School, Clacton-on-Sea

 # The Raindrop

When the raindrop fell
It brought happiness to me,
When I heard the bells
It was very clear to see,
My family were very happy
To see that it was true,
I had discovered that my heart is always with you.

Molly Carpenter (11)
Clacton County High School, Clacton-on-Sea

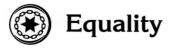 # Equality

Where have we come?
This perfect life?
We teach our children,
To be kind and generous.
However, somewhere,
Shackles lay on wrists.

Today, we look down,
Down our noses.
To people who are the same,
The same as us,
The only difference,
The colour of our skin.

Love thy neighbour,
You was taught the same.
Yet you betray your 'God',
You leave him astray.

We are people,
We are all the same,
No matter what you see.

Luke Dean Russell Corneloues
Clacton County High School, Clacton-on-Sea

 # Chocolate

Oh chocolate, so soft,
So smooth and silky.
My taste buds jump with joy
As you melt away.

Oh chocolate, so creamy,
So mouth-watering, so tasty
That Augustus couldn't keep
His hands off you.

Georgia Buxey (14)
Clacton County High School, Clacton-on-Sea

Everybody's Different!

Never be bullied into silence
Nor domestic violence.
Never be made to be a victim
Don't take criticism.

Everybody's different in many ways,
Don't let bullies make you pay.
All bullies are really bad,
Just remember deep down they're sad.

They all try to look the same,
All try to give themselves names.
All this wrong people do,
All because they're jealous of you.

When people say you're nothing,
Remember what to do.
Just sit back and smile and remember
There are others like you.

Jodie Field
Clacton County High School, Clacton-on-Sea

My Rights!

My life, my way, my rights, my parents' way,
My life, horrible.

My friends, they judge,
Bullies can't get enough.

My pain, broken heart,
My loss of friends.

My anger, my way.

My telling off, the teacher's way.

My anger is this way.

Alisha-Jade Dunning (11)
Clacton County High School, Clacton-on-Sea

School Is Bad

I hate school
Also the swimming pool
We have to follow rules
Which is not cool.

School is a bore
I would rather run into a door
They try to lure
You into this utter bore.

School is boring
I would rather be at home
Where I can be doing something
Playing on dome.

School is a bore
I would rather run into a door
They try to lure
You into this utter bore.

Kai Elliot Madden (12)
Clacton County High School, Clacton-on-Sea

Girls

I am a girl,
I like sports.
Yes, I can play football,
Yes, I can run,
But just because I'm a girl, it means I get judged.
Us girls can do everything you can
Just because we are girls doesn't mean that we can't do anything.
White, black, old and young
We are all equal.
So girls, don't be afraid to be yourself.
Be different.

Taylor Albert (13)
Clacton County High School, Clacton-on-Sea

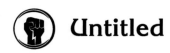

Untitled

I sit there wishing what could I be?
Sitting there wishing I could be free.
As my demons surrounds me,
In my thoughts it gives me pain
And I get filled with nothing but shame.
I want to be the best I can be
And block out the people that look down on me.
I wanna look down on my kingdom around
And show them I was more than a disappointment
And fight for what is right.
Work hard and have whatever you like,
Don't let people get you down,
If they do give them a bite.
I'm going to push these demons out of me
And I'm going to break free and be me
And no one's stopping me being the man
I've always wanted to be.

Harry Southwood (14)
Clacton County High School, Clacton-on-Sea

Dissimilis

D efender of the needy
I s never greedy
S mart without praise
S trong and brave
I can still feel fear
M y eyes cry with tears
I don't fit in
L et a change begin
I nside I know
S truggles will go

I am a Dissimilis.

Lacey Stonham (13)
Clacton County High School, Clacton-on-Sea

What's Really Going Through Her Mind?

On the outside she's laughing and smiling
But on the inside she's just crying.
She tried to tell you she was down.
Guess you didn't care.
Her big dull eyes
Are really a great disguise
To hide those sad feelings.
Bet you didn't know her scars are only slowly healing.
Every night she sits and cries
Those hurtful words will never leave her mind.
She wonders if anyone actually cares.
Everything you said, tearing her apart.
Just remember I'll be here for you whenever
We'll always be best friends forever
And I'm never really far.

Louise Lawrence (13)
Clacton County High School, Clacton-on-Sea

Success

Some people think things will just come to them,
But get to reality,
You need to work hard to achieve your dreams,
They don't just come off your sleeve,
You work every day
And think to yourself, *I can do this.*
People with negative minds, don't get a lot,
But people with positive minds
And attitudes push themselves
And one day you will realise
Your friends, family, teachers always say,
'Good things will come to the people who work for it.'

Tanya Costanzo (14)
Clacton County High School, Clacton-on-Sea

Crushed

As I think about the good times,
The bad times come charging through,
The way we were so close . . .
But then she came along.

Everything changed.
Everything was ruined
Even memories.

It left me in pieces
But you didn't care.
I had to build my confidence back up.
Alone!

You walked off laughing
While I was crying.

You made her proud
While you made me cry.

Jaide Leonard (12)
Clacton County High School, Clacton-on-Sea

 # My Life

Morning,
Eyes open,
School,
Intelligence,
Again failure,
Hard work,
Successful,
Job,
Silence,
All black,
Life over,
All over again.

Jason Lynch (13)
Clacton County High School, Clacton-on-Sea

Missing My Best Friend

I wipe a tear from my eye
Just thinking about you, makes my heart crumble.
I hate when you say bye
When I walk down the stairs I tumble
But you saved me.
I close my eyes, and think
You told me that if any boy comes between us
We will still be best friends.
You're on a date, and I'm there
And he told me to go away.
I went home and cried,
She asked him where I went.
He said, 'She wanted to go home.'
'Don't be with him!' I shouted.
'If you're not being there, then you're not my friend,' she replied.
I didn't see her for five years and I still remember.

Hailie Fenech (11)
Clacton County High School, Clacton-on-Sea

Mystery Girl

I noticed in a playground
A girl by herself.
She was lonely,
She sang a lot before.
Don't really see her sing anymore.

She is different now!
She's got friends,
She's not lonely anymore
Because I am . . .

I am the one in the playground by myself,
Looking around singing to myself.
I am the lonely one . . .

Paige Ibbotson (14)
Clacton County High School, Clacton-on-Sea

We Care

Every day someone needs help
But someone just says no
Every day someone's in need
People just say no
But one day when they need help
We will say yes
Because when that day comes
They will be in our care.

Every day someone is hurt
People do not help
Every day someone cries
People just walk away
When people need our help
We will be there
Any time of the day.

Jamie-Moore Langley (14)
Clacton County High School, Clacton-on-Sea

Roses

Roses are red
That much is true,
But violets are purple
Not actually blue.

Roses are white
Like the moon is at night.
But it's sooo pretty,
What a sight.

Roses are blue,
Wait, no they're not.
Neither are violets
So I lie a lot.

Charlie Jay Phillips (13)
Clacton County High School, Clacton-on-Sea

Random

I don't like it here
It smells like beer
I sometimes see lots of deer.

I'm only three
But I'm an expert at climbing trees
My favourite things are bees
I like to eat a lot of peas.

I like going on my bike
Once at school we went for a hike
I pricked myself on a spike.

I like the word school
It rhymes with stool
My mum says I'm cool
My nan lets me in her paddling pool.

Robbie Jay (12)
Clacton County High School, Clacton-on-Sea

Through The Glass Eye

The dew lay early in the day
Where I lay my glass eye stays
Moving angels to see how I play.
Men watch through the glass eye
To see my arguments through the day,
I try to turn it off but it will stay.
My glass eye loses energy throughout the day.
On my bed I will stay until the men will go away.

The men will watch until I say . . .
No more power throughout the day!
My phone will stay on my bed until the men go . . .
Away!

Kofi (13)
Clacton County High School, Clacton-on-Sea

The Big Part Of My Heart!

He's a big part in my heart,
Known by most people in the world.
The most caring person on Earth.

Loving, caring, powerful.

He is with us every day,
He could be a big part of your heart,
Loving us all the time,
Cheering us up when we cry.

Loving, caring, powerful.

Answering our prayers,
He could be in our hearts,
He gives us hope.

He is Jesus.

Xena Martin (12)
Clacton County High School, Clacton-on-Sea

1986 - Chernobyl

In 1986 there was a nuclear explosion,
It shocked Ukraine in devastation.
The nuclear gas spread around,
It made Pripyat all upside down.
Reactor 4 blew up in a bang,
The nuclear gas turned into toxic rain.
25 years later, Pripyat
Is still under attack, by Mother Nature ripping walls.
You wouldn't like to be on your own,
The things that would rot, are your bones
By nuclear gas.

Nathan Smith (13)
Clacton County High School, Clacton-on-Sea

Friends

I hope the relationship never ends
Between me and my best friend
We do everything together
And will do forever
Me and my best friend
She's not just my best friend
She is also like my sister
Before any mister
Me and my best friend
I love her loads
And loads and loads
And millions of trillions
Me and my best friend
And I hope the relationship never ends
Between me and my best friend.

Clare Rose
Clacton County High School, Clacton-on-Sea

Broken Country

Living in this broken country,
Where people starve and go hungry,
I really need some food,
To improve my mood.
In this damaged society,
People just sit quietly
And let the Queen
Be really mean.
Wars and fighting,
When will this end?
Hopefully, this broken country will mend.

Elysia Cordrey (12)
Clacton County High School, Clacton-on-Sea

Oh Sweet God

Oh sweet God
I'm too good,
Better than you,
Like violets are blue.
You wish You could
Be this good,
Unlucky mate,
Need some practise?
What a sweat,
That's me
The FIFA threat.
Oh sweet God
What have I done?
Beaten you at FIFA,
Get down son!

Ollie Palmer (13)
Clacton County High School, Clacton-on-Sea

Stop Bullying

Don't call people names
Because it will come back in your face,
If you are upset
And mad with yourself,
People commit suicide every day
Because of people like you,
Why you got to be so mean,
Why are you so jealous?
Because they're going to be more liked than you,
They are strong not like you,
They don't take their anger out on you.

Mia Luck (11)
Clacton County High School, Clacton-on-Sea

My Issue Today . . .

My issue today is the time that I pay
Wasting it all on homework
We spend time at school (five hours in fact)
It's so we don't fall
Off the cliff that is life
But back to the issue at hand
I know this topic has some fans
But I don't see why we need homework
It's as useless as no work
At the end of the day
The teachers should pay!
For not making time to teach us . . .
This was my point
And I'm not blaming it on teachers
I'm saying there is no point.

Wesley Laing
Clacton County High School, Clacton-on-Sea

 # We . . .

We are born, we grow, we learn, we evolve,
We kill . . . we are born, it dies, we die . . .
We grow, it dies, we die . . . we learn, it dies,
We die . . . we evolve, it dies, we die . . .

We are born, we grow, we learn, we evolve,
We help . . . we are born, it lives, we live . . .
We grow, it lives, we live . . . we learn,
It lives, we live . . . we evolve, it lives, we live.

We kill, we help, it dies, it lives,
We die, we live . . . why?

Lee Revell (12)
Clacton County High School, Clacton-on-Sea

Kind World

I see blue skies most places I go,
Sometimes I feel in my head a rainbow,
Different colours for different feelings,
I wonder, they may have some unusual meanings.

Kindness is one of the things people love
And natural things like a pure white dove,
Smiles on your face,
Fun personality,
The world follows your ways.

The world counts on your style
Like a dog counts on your love,
Make yourself known as an uplifting person.
One more thing for you to know,
We are a kind world.

Stevie Steel (13)
Clacton County High School, Clacton-on-Sea

Patience

Patience boy, patience . . .
That's the words I'll hear,
Sit back and relax
The day it comes is very near.
Patience boy, patience . . .
Follow rules, pay the tax,
Pass the time, drink some beer
Get hungover, forget the facts.
Patience boy, patience . . .
The mailman knocks, it is here!
I do not know, the speaker's at max
Too busy partying, not getting that gear.
Time for waiting . . .
Patience boy, patience.

Bailey Prior
Clacton County High School, Clacton-on-Sea

My Special Friend

I have a friend and my friend's name is Lilly.
She isn't like all my other friends because she is special to me.
As I skateboard along on the beach
And she runs behind me.
I can see joy in her face
As she runs quickly to catch me up.
As we come to a halt I see her panting like mad
In front of my eyes I can't help but laugh a little bit.
As I start pushing off again
I can see her go zooming past me with the wind in her hair.
We are getting near the end,
Now just a couple more pushes and then we're done.
We come to the end and I put my dog Lilly's lead on
And we're done for another day.

Haydn Robinson (12)
Clacton County High School, Clacton-on-Sea

 # Thoughts

To make someone feel upset, alone,
Like they have nothing and no one.

It isn't funny,
And it definitely doesn't make you look hard.

But it is horrible
And it is disrespectful.

So don't care about what your friends think.
Try and impress the people around you, everyone!

So for once stop what you're doing and think . . .

Zoe Faye Dore (13)
Clacton County High School, Clacton-on-Sea

Bullying

Even if your best friend
Is getting bullied
Don't join the crowd
Like some people would.

Stick up for them!
Race in like a bullet
And save them from the horrible crowd
Because they are like a flower,
They can fade away!
Don't lose them!

Kirsty McNeilly (11)
Clacton County High School, Clacton-on-Sea

Trapped

Being trapped
And told what to do
Isn't the world we should be living in anymore.
Being afraid isn't something we should be feeling anymore.

Stand up for yourself.
Tell them it isn't right.
Stand up for yourself,
But don't start a fight.
Stand up for your feelings,
Tell them how you're feeling.

Megan Greet (13)
Clacton County High School, Clacton-on-Sea

First Sight

The first kiss upon the lips felt absolutely bright
As if the clouds under decided to be light.
Butterflies from stomach to toes fluttered with the wind.
As hands locked, connected like this was infinite.
Pure heart and soul; never loved before
It was true magic
I tell you, nothing seen before.
The miss from the heart bled like never-ending
But soon it would stop,
Heal with true love's sending.

Cece Le Roux (14)
Clacton County High School, Clacton-on-Sea

Peace

I look for peace
If there was no war
The world would be peaceful.

I believe in kindness and love
Everybody deserves a second chance
Why can't we be as peaceful as a dove?

If we were to love, we would be free,
I look for hope
Just like the Pope.

Liam Leech (13)
Clacton County High School, Clacton-on-Sea

Thy Deep Blue

As delicate as a diamond the waves do glide
Atlantis falling long and still.
The fresh sea breeze
Drifting across the golden sand stretched bay.

The ocean's hurting but care we not
Make Mother Nature boiling hot.
The polar caps are melting, the wildlife is disappearing
So in years to come when your children ask what happened to this place,
Remember you chose not to help save our home.

Billie-Anne Crew (13)
Clacton County High School, Clacton-on-Sea

 # Benevolenha

You're the one I love the most,
The one who's always with me.

People call me your friend,
I relate to you as a sister.

Our friendship is like a magnet
That can never come apart.

Yours sincerely,
From your best friend.

Kacey George (12)
Clacton County High School, Clacton-on-Sea

 # Different

I am different,
I know I am,
It's what makes people special,
If everyone's normal it would be boring,
This is where I come in,
I do things weird and exciting,
Sometimes I'm normal,
But I get bored,
This is why I'm different!

Alex Cook (12)
Clacton County High School, Clacton-on-Sea

 # Monster

You try your hardest to fight,
But the light is just too bright,
Then you take a turn for the worst,
You change into the monster,
The monster that will show,
But there comes a time where you just stop . . .
Think . . . and grow,
Grow until you show,
Show who you are.

Tyler Staples (13)
Clacton County High School, Clacton-on-Sea

Rise To Fall

It ends here
The cycle has been persistent
As time flies
I fall . . .
Wounds of words cover my emotional body
Slowly becoming worse
My only highs are climbing
So they can make me fall again
End the cycle.

Jake Ware (14)
Clacton County High School, Clacton-on-Sea

 # Untitled

Do you know what we go through,
Parents and teachers getting in our way,
Every day I find something to say,
But it's the same every day.

It's hard being me,
Freedom is all I plead,
I just want to go away
With my phone to play.

Sophie Ballard
Clacton County High School, Clacton-on-Sea

Red Mist

Yes it is angering,
No you can't hit.
Yes it is frustrating,
No you can't kick.
For all it is worth,
Your enemy is weak.
For all it may hurt
Keep your anger hidden deep.

Michael David Anthony Johnson (13)
Clacton County High School, Clacton-on-Sea

 # War

In a cold, dark desert
There was war everywhere
War, war, will you die
Or will you survive?
Will you care
Or will you share?
Stop, stop the war
Because you will become poor.

Casey Warren-Haynes (13)
Clacton County High School, Clacton-on-Sea

 # Everyone's Different

We cry, we smile
We all laugh in pain
We cry, we smile
We sing all day.

Holly Francis (12)
Clacton County High School, Clacton-on-Sea

The Castitas

The world has a hole and I fall the most
I try not to be distressed when I am the host
The ghost of my past haunts me
The demon of my future mocks me
Alone in my hole I scrape some sanity
Alone in my hole, alone in me
Leave me be
In my hole.

Jake Ware (14)
Clacton County High School, Clacton-on-Sea

Poverty

A current affair is poverty
It should not happen
We should all respect with loyalty
But this can happen horribly
So let's get together and fix this mess
That has made these people stressed
Let's get their lives back
And put them back on track.

Kieran Garside
Clacton County High School, Clacton-on-Sea

Dissmilis

The happiness makes my hands and aims
Twist and turn in a majestic state of no control
The anger makes my bones shake
And my head spins in an unusual sequence.

Sophie Ballard
Clacton County High School, Clacton-on-Sea

Land Of Death

Standing in a land of death
Crimes like robbery and theft,
It's easier to think positive thoughts
Than to sit alone feeling distraught.
Sitting alone extremely tired
Listening to all the gunshots being fired.
These people are not to blame
For this war of hurt and shame.

Ella Hern (13)
Clacton County High School, Clacton-on-Sea

PlayStation . . .

PlayStation is the best,
PlayStation beats the rest,
The rest will never be the best,
Because the best is better than the rest,
So PS4 will always be the best,
The Xbox is one of the rest
So it will never be the best.

Connor Hickey (14)
Clacton County High School, Clacton-on-Sea

I Care

I care about you
You care about me
We care about each other like a buddy
We like to hug, we like to eat
We care about each other like family.

Bethany Darvill Cutts (12)
Clacton County High School, Clacton-on-Sea

Temperantia

Sometimes they're kind
Sometimes they're mean
They're always there
Just look behind
Laughing and giggling
Taking the mick
Just bullies they are.

Samuel Russell (11)
Clacton County High School, Clacton-on-Sea

Dissimilis

A lonely road on a summer's day,
No cars drive by, no horse or hay.

The rain comes down, the cold appears,
No warming hug comes near.

No shelter for the needy,
Only love for the greedy.

Sabrina Liddard
Clacton County High School, Clacton-on-Sea

Dissimilis

I like my dog when he runs,
Panting along when I'm getting my fitness up,
But then again it might be fun,
Running along the sand,
Running out of air on my way home,
Giving the dog a bath.

Keelan Gearey (11)
Clacton County High School, Clacton-on-Sea

Humilitas

In a meadow a young girl sat,
Her hair golden and eyes sky-blue.

The daisy chain within her fingers,
Represents her loving heart.

Her hair swayed in the lukewarm wind
And her eyes glisten in the bright red, beaming sun.

Georgia Buisson
Clacton County High School, Clacton-on-Sea

 # Peace Poem

I help people.
I don't ask for anything in return.
I do it because I get a buzz out of helping people.
I very rarely get anything out of it.
I want peace.
I hope this war stops before I drop . . .

Finley Caro (13)
Clacton County High School, Clacton-on-Sea

Mum And Dad

I wish it didn't happen
I don't want to feel the pain anymore
If only I was younger
So I didn't have to hear it for myself
It took time to calm down
Just hope one day everything will be the same again.

Holly Heath (12)
Clacton County High School, Clacton-on-Sea

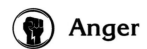
Anger

Fight me, fight me
So I lose all the anger
Dying inside, and crying on the out.
Keep my hand away
From your face.
So my feelings will never embrace.

Hallie French (11)
Clacton County High School, Clacton-on-Sea

Happiness Is The Truth

Oh banana, what a treat you are,
A food from above.
A best friend with porridge
And one of your 5-a-day.
Oh banana, how could anyone live without you.
You're a part of all our lives.

Liam McCarthy (11)
Clacton County High School, Clacton-on-Sea

Being The Boss!

Being successful is all I need.
I don't need anyone to tell me what to do
Because I am the one to get to the top,
I start as a rookie
And work to be the boss!

Robert Williams (12)
Clacton County High School, Clacton-on-Sea

Let The Haters Hate

If your best friend is having a fight
Don't join the crowd,
Help if you are a true friend
Because that's what a true friend is
Even if it means being hated.

Sean Hall (11)
Clacton County High School, Clacton-on-Sea

 # Untitled

We cry, we laugh
We all are together
Every single day.
We sing every day
We cry, we laugh.

Sophia Boughey
Clacton County High School, Clacton-on-Sea

Bonnie And Clyde

Rhett was a b*****d
Scarett a bitch
Romeo and Juliet naive
Helena slept all over Greece
And made a whole city flee
The greatest love stories of our time
Show us only the powerful get to love

When the hot sun beats, sweep her off her feet
Woo her away from the bore of the day
Into adventure, loss and laughs
A fierce world embedded with heart
Where you'll argue like politicians
And make love like animals

Fast cars, fast world and a fast love
A world of fury and want
Slow people, slow days and slow nights
A world of serious bite

Like an old comedy show
Your life will go
Full of farce situations and seriousness
And though the world may get thinner
And the lights dimmer and dimmer
You'll ignore all the sin that you'll commit
And turn your heads from Death's list
Where your names are in capitals
With wish next to it

And though you are no Bennet or Darcy
Your love is as big as those names
You'll challenge life, you'll challenge the game
Surrounded by adventure and grief

Though you may part with an almighty tat
The laughs and the love will not fall flat
And you'll look back into the past
With a smile and gleam
How you challenged the world in one small dream

Though you aren't thought of like Antony and Cleo
As you topple onto Death's soft pillow
You'll smile and think, someone looked through the grime
And found your love, tested by time
Cemented by crime

And they'll realise love doesn't just belong to those few
Star-crossed lovers surrounded by riches
Love is for all those ready to take the manic ride
And fly to the moon

That's why I want to be Bonnie and Clyde.

Adam George Jezard (18)
East Norfolk Sixth Form College, Great Yarmouth

 # I Have Not Got A Single Clue - Haiku

Oh, what shall I do?
I don't have a single clue,
Oh please, oh please, help.

Bethany Francis (12)
Great Yarmouth (VA) High School, Great Yarmouth

The Honey Badger

I eat snakes for breakfast
I devour my own kind for tea
Mankind is my pupil
Nobody can tame me.

I am fiercer than a dragon
But as small as a monkey
I am as strong as a gorilla
And I am part of the weasel family.

I am hated by lions
I am feared by snakes
I make grown bears cry
And my heart never aches.

I am the smartest animal on the planet
But I do sometimes rage
Give me a stick and you'll see
I can escape any cage.

I . . .
Am . . .
The . . .
Honey badger.

Harry Slater (11)
Great Yarmouth (VA) High School, Great Yarmouth

Balloon

Your love is a balloon,
Makes a smile when seen,
Flies endlessly around the world
And raises me up.

Sends me happiness and joy,
Making everyone see,
That you are free,
And can fly ever so joyfully.

Not desperate for attention,
No need for sympathy,
Just glowing faces,
Shining so brightly.

Some days you fall down,
But rise up, back again,
Always going through clouds,
And floating among the stars.

Night, day, sun, rain,
You can go through anything,
Battling down against wind and clouds,
Your journey's a destiny.

Your love is a balloon,
Makes a smile when seen,
Flies endlessly around the world
And raises me up . . .

So high like a balloon.

Ria Mae Bedford (12)
Great Yarmouth (VA) High School, Great Yarmouth

The Psycho

The psycho cuts out another picture
Sticks it on her wall,
Goes onto Twitter, follows every tweet
Waiting to hear more.

She's planned it very carefully
Since many days before,
Picks up her key, picks up her purse
And goes out of the door.

The psycho has finally found him
She's been watching him since six,
Under her breath, she's mumbling
And her body's all a-twitch.

He's left the building he was in
But she had left it first,
The wheels on his sports car spin
Leaving her to curse.

The psycho wanders to her home
Thinking about that night,
Get home, checks his Facebook page
Says, 'Rocked that concert tonight'.

The fan girl cuts out another picture
Sticks it on her wall.
Goes onto Twitter, follows every tweet,
Waiting to hear more.

Cameron Gibbs (12)
Great Yarmouth (VA) High School, Great Yarmouth

 # Gay Rights!

Yes, he's gay
So what?
I don't care.

Allow his lungs to at least breathe the same air.

If you don't like it
So long,
Farewell!

It would probably do him just as well
Just as long as you're gone and out of his sight
Then he'll be able to sleep at night.

Imagine a world the other way round,
If you were straight
You wouldn't make a sound.

Think about that when he passes in the hall
'Ha gay!'
Up gays!
Yay for gay rights!'

Stand up for them today, tomorrow
and the rest of your life!

You may be straight,
What you're doing isn't right!

Leah Cantillon (13)
Great Yarmouth (VA) High School, Great Yarmouth

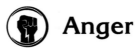 **Anger**

Anger.
Like boiling water in an oil tank
A ticking time bomb
Waiting to explode.

Ignorance, broken dreams
And no respect.
Filling up anger tanks
Bubbling like a stove.

Hearing screams in my head,
Blurring out reality
But finally the pin drops
And in rushes the anger.

Inexplicable rage,
Friends turn into adversaries.
Violence overcoming peace,
Anger surging through my veins.
But the engine cools off
To a deserted room
And I think *what happened?*
But it's only anger.

Joseph Storey (11)
Great Yarmouth (VA) High School, Great Yarmouth

 **The Ice**

I am the ice that makes you fall over
Even the rain can't stop me from forming
I make it so hard to drive your car
I double the chance to crash in your car
I even can stop you opening your door
You try to stop me with hot water
It's no use, I'm here to stay.

Ben Brown (12)
Great Yarmouth (VA) High School, Great Yarmouth

Bully

People all around you
Always have something to say
Whether it's nice or not
Never listen to them
What they do or say can be as nasty as a punch.
Don't let them know it hurts you,
It's not true.
Nobody is perfect,
Ignore it.
It's easier said than done,
If you don't tell anyone
It could go too far,
Let people know
Get help
It will get better
The bullies will learn,
Get a punishment
You are brilliant,
Even if it's not said enough.

Nicole Hrabec-Lunn (12)
Great Yarmouth (VA) High School, Great Yarmouth

The Python

My anger's like the python, a train of scales
Which travels in the grass which are its own green tracks.

And its dagger-like teeth
That bite its victim
Contains the venom which is like a poison apple.

Its eyes are written with death
As they glow as red as blood
While it slithers along with a mouth having a venom flood.

Jack Church (12)
Great Yarmouth (VA) High School, Great Yarmouth

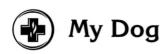
My Dog

My dog, Roxy, hogs all of the bones.
Her teeth are so strong
She could eat a bunch of stones.
She is small and brown just like an oak tree.
Every time at night she wants my KFC.
Her eyes are big, I bet she can see the moon
Or I think they're big because her head is as big as a spoon.
She is lazy and fat just like a cat.
She nicks all the food and acts like a dude.
She thinks she owns the house
And we are the slaves.
All she does is wee on the cat's grave.
She is brave and mighty,
She likes to get in fights,
She is like an Xpro knight.
As she is getting older she is getting very slow
Now she is losing her Xpro.
As she is getting weak she stays in her cage,
And waits for her life to turn the next page.

Alex Crowe (11)
Great Yarmouth (VA) High School, Great Yarmouth

 # The Fog

The fog is a mysterious spectre,
Wonderful in many ways,
Covering nature's beautiful sights,
Hiding it away for days.

Blanketing the high green hill,
Taking it from our sight,
Cloaking the valleys low,
With no effect, with no might.

Adam Hart (11)
Great Yarmouth (VA) High School, Great Yarmouth

Emotions

Peace is the open door for sorrow
Turning on the light
Helping people with choices
Making the pathway bright.

Love is the light to the heart of Heaven
A completely different world
When you love someone keep them close
Like a precious pearl.

Hate is the mood from Hell
If you hate you'll feel down
You will be influenced by Satan
No happiness will come around.

Sorrow is the ocean that never ends
When you go on in you may not come out
Sadness is deep and ever so wide
Once you experience this
You won't be the same I doubt.

Abbie Boast (11)
Great Yarmouth (VA) High School, Great Yarmouth

Valentines

V ery much I love you - that's how much
A lot perhaps
L oads even
E ven more than I love my puppies
N o one can change you in my heart
T o everyone - I really love him so much
I nside my heart - only you darling . . .
N othing is more important than you
E ven more than I love The Vamps
S o you really love me darling.

Sania Mavia Gusmao (13)
Great Yarmouth (VA) High School, Great Yarmouth

Thinking Of You

Can't believe that you're leaving
Leaving me behind
But I'll never forget you
'Cause you've always been kind

Thinking of you every day of my life
Thinking of you
We will always be together forever
I'll be thinking of you

Please don't leave me alone
Please don't let this end
But I'll never forget you
Cos you're the best of my friends

Thinking of you every day of my life
Thinking of you
We will always be together forever
I'll be thinking of you.

Cassandra Smith (12)
Great Yarmouth (VA) High School, Great Yarmouth

Valentine's Day

V alentine's Day
A nother day to stuff your face and watch chick flicks
L ying about waiting for your prince in shining armour
E ating Ben & Jerry's
N ot a care in the world
T ogether we could be, forever
I nstead I'm all alone
N ever leave me alone
E verything is perfect
S ome dread this day but with you I know however far apart, you're always
   in my heart.

Kaitee Miller (11)
Great Yarmouth (VA) High School, Great Yarmouth

Winter Is A Witch

Winter is a witch,
Casting spells on Earth.
Showering hail down upon us,
As it whispers its deadly curse.

Lakes freeze at its arrival
Causing danger to little locals.
As the witch finishes her trap
The victims scream their vocals.

Freezing weather in its cauldron,
Sends chills to the humans.
It sends shivers through the human's body,
From feet to head to hands.

It travels around the world;
Even Australia gets a numbing,
But when it finishes with down under,
You know winter is coming . . .

Sapphire Michelle Hodgkyns (12)
Great Yarmouth (VA) High School, Great Yarmouth

Fighting The Darkness

I am lost
Under the black seas
My eyes are gone
I can't see the light
My mind is in pain
I think about other people's feelings
I can't control myself
I try to fight the darkness
But they are controlling my mind
I try to stop it but nothing is working
I keep falling down, I can't get back up.

Edi Silva (13)
Great Yarmouth (VA) High School, Great Yarmouth

Bad Temper

A man who has a really bad temper,
Looked all pale and grey,
If someone knocked on his door,
He would get quite annoyed.

Not even the bogeyman would attack him,
He was too afraid,
No one went near him,
He was all alone.

Until one day, a letter popped,
Right through his door.
It said that he was to be
Sent to another planet.

So up on board is where he popped,
And off to Mars he went,
Two years so far, has he been there,
Dead? Well, we do not know?

Daniel Sanderson (12)
Great Yarmouth (VA) High School, Great Yarmouth

 # Valentines

V ery much I love you
A lot perhaps
L ife is to enjoy
E njoy love
N o one can take you away from me!
T ons of chocolates and flowers
I t's impossible for me to love you even more
N ever ever going to take you away
E veryone loves you on Valentine's Day
S eriously love you.

Maisy Doole (12)
Great Yarmouth (VA) High School, Great Yarmouth

The Fog

I am the fog.
I am much worse than ghosts and vampires,
I'm always hanging around on the cold, breezy ground
I'm never up, always down.
I feast on your eyes
As you can't really see cos it's me
And you know I'm after you.
You never know if I'm here or not,
You hardly see me a lot and when you do,
You can't bear me anymore
As you can't really see.
I'm every bad thing put together,
I'm no doubt by far the worst weather,
You'll always hate it when I'm here.
Take one more look at me, no?
Because you can't really see.

Harry Smith (11)
Great Yarmouth (VA) High School, Great Yarmouth

The City

The city is alive at night,
Lighting the city's surroundings with the brightest of lights,
Never sleeping, always thriving,
The movement, never dying.

The moon and the stars are nothing,
Compared to the lights that are shining,
You can spot this phenomenon from miles away,
But one thing will not delay.

The beautiful sunset set in the background,
Watching over the city, lying on the ground,
The city has now awoken at the crack of dawn,
At last, a new day has been born.

Kacey Halstead (12)
Great Yarmouth (VA) High School, Great Yarmouth

I Am The Sea

I am the sea
I calmly lay on the rocky shores
As sweetly as can be
All I want is for people to have fun.

However I have a rough side
And if I don't like you then good luck on this ride
I hate to harm but oh I am so salty
That even the sourest of people all go to hide
I am the sea, as different as can be.

As I swallow the grainy sand
I feel a tiny little hand
It belonged to a small tender child
Oh how I felt with so much sorrow
But I had no choice
He had to go to the bottom of the pile.

Kaci Elaine White (12)
Great Yarmouth (VA) High School, Great Yarmouth

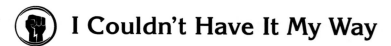

I Couldn't Have It My Way

There's nothing else to say. I couldn't have it my way.
He screamed in horror. He screamed in pain.
He struggled, he wriggled, I laughed, I giggled.
He knew he'd have to pay, I couldn't have it my way.

He saw no more light of day, I couldn't have it my way.
I felt no guilt. I felt but gay.
For sure, he was dead, his blood, but red.
Under my bed he lay, I couldn't have it my way.

His skin, like clay, I couldn't have it my way.
In an unseen sack, carried down to the bay.
I loosened my grip, and he took a dip.
There's nothing else to say, I couldn't have it my way.

Mia Hudson (11)
Great Yarmouth (VA) High School, Great Yarmouth

 # Cake

I am like a cake,
I'm soft and pokey,
I can look sweet sometimes,
My insides bake when I get hot,
Some people like me, others don't,
I can get sickly,
If you take too much you'll get a bellyache,
When I get hot I will start to burn,
Decorate me and make me look pretty,
If you add the wrong ingredients things will go wrong,
Many people like me, some don't
People always talk about me,
I'm very noticeable,
I smell nice,
I've got many ingredients to make me who I am!

Chloe Bellingham (11)
Great Yarmouth (VA) High School, Great Yarmouth

 # The Weather

I'm the weather,
On days I can be as light as a feather
Wind me up and I'll bring rain,
Wind, cold, storms and pain.

I control the world,
People fear me,
I'll change in a flash,
From calm to rough
And you'll have a gash.

Many people love me when I bring sun
You may sunbathe and your kids will have fun
Summer's time for sunscreen and lying on the beach
It's the summer holidays - you don't need to teach.

Harry Young (12)
Great Yarmouth (VA) High School, Great Yarmouth

My Nature Poem

Moving with elegance,
Yet ever so slow,
I let the wind guide me,
Swaying to and fro,
Every day I lose a bright green leaf,
They fall to the ground,
Then get kicked by feet.
If I'm in a forest,
We lose someone every day
Men with sharp weapons
Chop and take them away
I'm just part of nature
I give oxygen to breathe
So please, please, please
Don't kill us trees!

Meghan Rhianne Chloe Spencer-Sanders (12)
Great Yarmouth (VA) High School, Great Yarmouth

Wetting Your Day!

I am the rain hitting down on people
Always there even if you try to escape
I make people feel sad and darken their day
I keep you inside so you can't play.

You can try to get rid of me I always come back
Lurking on the corners waiting to wet your day
I make you run home to hide
But you can't hide there forever
You think you're safe but you're not.

I'm waiting for the right chance to get you
You think that your day is sunny but just wait
People dare to leave their homes
For I would get them straight away.

Georgia Alley (12)
Great Yarmouth (VA) High School, Great Yarmouth

The Boy

My heart pounded as I saw his green eyes,
Shining in the sunlight,
His soft hair blowing in the breeze,
He turns his head towards me,
Taking slow steps he gets closer and closer,
He looks me in the eye,
I'm dying on the spot,
I fall to the ground, everything goes black,
I wake up in my bed,
Was it just a dream?
Well that's what I think,
Until I see him, the gorgeous boy,
Sat next to my bed,
'Hi I'm Josh.'

Ellie-May Rankine (12)
Great Yarmouth (VA) High School, Great Yarmouth

Turn That Frown Upside Down

If life gets you down
Turn that frown upside down

When I am sad . . .
I eat ten cream eclairs
I call nine of my friends and ask how their day was
I watch eight funny videos on YouTube
I learn seven new songs
I organise six parties
I learn five new words
I repeat four elements from the periodic table
I ask for three hugs
I clean two rooms in my house
I can now say I am one happy person.

Zoe McCullough (13)
Great Yarmouth (VA) High School, Great Yarmouth

⭕ Seagulls

A seagull is like ten starving pigs
In a six-foot ditch
And the only source of food is mud and worms.

They look for a long time
For a delicious warm snack
Taking your food out of your hands.

Flying off to eat your food
While babies are sad
Without food they start to cry, 'Mom!'

And dads buy babies more,
Now they're laughing
With grins on their faces.

Abbie Humphreys (11)
Great Yarmouth (VA) High School, Great Yarmouth

 I Am A . . .

I am a lightbulb
Always looking over people's shoulders
You know when I'm happy
I am everywhere.

I am lurking in the dark
Hiding so no one can see me
My personality can be changed
I light up like the sun.

I brighten up your day
You will always need me
I'll never go away
You could break me.

Keeley Smalley (12)
Great Yarmouth (VA) High School, Great Yarmouth

The Sea Is A Dog

The sea is a vicious dog
Gnawing at a juicy bone,
His teeth as sharp as daggers
Thoughts of being at home.
He protects what's his with all his might
Not letting anyone see,
His face in his thin-haired paws
With thoughts like, *God help me.*
His head is spinning
He's overthinking
What is he going to do
With thoughts like, *I'm coming back for you.*

Rebecca Cole (11)
Great Yarmouth (VA) High School, Great Yarmouth

Oh Pasta

Oh pasta,
You are the only thing I love,
You light up the skies,
Without you,
My meals will never be the same,
Oh pasta,
I wish the world,
Was made out of you,
That will be my version of Heaven,
Oh pasta, oh pasta,
I love you more than life itself,
Also you taste nice with meatballs.

Aaron Bassett (11)
Great Yarmouth (VA) High School, Great Yarmouth

Valentine's Day

V alentine's Day
A ll you do is sit down
L azing around
E ating junk food
N ot a care in the world
T ogether you could be forever
I know you love him
N ever let him down
E very day you dream he's thinking about you
S omeday you'll find him and you will know that he is the one.

Alice Higgins (12)
Great Yarmouth (VA) High School, Great Yarmouth

Can't Find It

I will never find it,
My room, a mess,
I am stressed,
Can I find it?
No.

My room is a mess,
Not litter, just chaos,
I must confess,
I can't see all of it,
I won't find it.

Adam Easey (13)
Great Yarmouth (VA) High School, Great Yarmouth

The Feeling Of Love

The feeling of the warm hugs
The touch of the lips
A shivering sensation travelling down your back
The feeling of love
Never felt a feeling like this
Never felt like a home
He is my universe
My galaxy
And I'm proud to call him
My own.

Teegan Donoghue (12)
Great Yarmouth (VA) High School, Great Yarmouth

Untitled

Hey I always loved you
Now don't leave me
I have nothing to live for
All I wanted was you
I rushed to see you
And you did not give me an answer
I had dreams about you
I never forgot you.

Andrew Harding (14)
Great Yarmouth (VA) High School, Great Yarmouth

Running

Legs move faster
Breathing gets heavier
Arms move quicker
Expectations get higher
The line gets closer
Hearts beat faster
The crowd gets louder
The medal around my neck.

Poppy Wynes (12)
Great Yarmouth (VA) High School, Great Yarmouth

What Am I?

I am the most powerful emotion of them all,
I am great but not tall.
I could end up with a ring on a finger,
Sometimes I'm not there for too long, I don't always linger.
You find me between boy and girl,
I always make people's hearts whirl.
A common saying is 'there is a twinkle in your eye',
But what am I?

Lula Smith
Great Yarmouth (VA) High School, Great Yarmouth

Love

L ove you all year, all day with all my heart
O h love, why can it be like this?
V ery hard but always there to help
E ven at the end, love you always, everywhere, until the end of my life.

Mariana Damasio (14)
Great Yarmouth (VA) High School, Great Yarmouth

Love!

Love, what is it?
Is it happiness or is it heart-breaking?
Love is confusing, love is hard
Why can't we just all get along!
Love, how is it?
Is it wonderful or is it dull?
I don't understand it
My head is going to explode.

Emily Turrell (12)
Great Yarmouth (VA) High School, Great Yarmouth

Life As A Teenager

Life as a teenager is really hard
Not about playing cards
We've got to work and get good grades
Even if we don't get paid
Life as a teenager is really hard
Some people want to end it fast
But maybe being a teenager won't be too hard.

Sharna Ford-Busson (12)
Great Yarmouth (VA) High School, Great Yarmouth

Chin

There was a young lady
Whose chin resembled the point of a pin
So she had it made sharp
And purchased a harp
And played several tunes with her chin.

Shinia McKenzie (11)
Great Yarmouth (VA) High School, Great Yarmouth

Polly And Molly

There once was a girl called Polly
She had a good friend called Molly
They fell down a hole
And went into a roll
And you always found them at Dolly's.

Natasha Taylor (11)
Great Yarmouth (VA) High School, Great Yarmouth

 # Untitled

Roses are red, violets are blue
I think we can make beautiful music together, don't you?
Every day, I find myself thinking about you.

Bethany Channell
Great Yarmouth (VA) High School, Great Yarmouth

Sumatran Tigers: Tiger Vs Man

The cruel hunters are triumphing,
While Sumatran tigers are on the brink of extinction.
This so-called 'orange terror of the jungle'
Illegally hunted for its precious fur,
Is shot, *bang, bang!* by greedy hunters on a regular basis.
There are now only 400 tigers left in Sumatra,
And that number is decreasing rapidly every year.
In ten years the critically endangered Sumatran tiger could be extinct
If people don't do anything about it.
Wildlife conservationists, as brave as lions,
Have been patrolling the forest daily,
Removing harsh snares and painful traps.

But the conservationists need more funds
To keep the patrols going,
So, are we going to help save the Sumatran tiger?

Or are we going to let it join the large group of extinct animals, like the dodo,
Sabre-toothed cat, cave lion, woolly mammoth, megalodon . . .

Connor Regan (12)
Parkside Pupil Referral Unit, Ipswich

 # Me

Me.
A teen.
A 12-year-old teen.
A 12-year-old teen who's about to be 13.
A teen that loves make-up.
A teen that has a sister.
A teen that loves hanging out with her friends.
A teen that loves their family.
A teen that loves going to Canada.
A teen.
Me.

Jethursini Mathipalarajah (13)
St Benedict's Catholic College, Colchester

N.A.U.S.E.A

What do we have here?
Six random girls.
Why even are they here?
Because they have something in common.

What do you mean?
Explain it to me.

Well . . .

Natalie is the love lunatic,
She loves a nice smile.
It could be a random stranger,
Or someone she's known for a while.
But anywhere she sets foot,
Awkwardness would be right behind her.

AJ, now here's a weird one,
She doesn't like being wrong.
She doesn't like being in arguments or fights
Oh well, that's life!
But anywhere she sets foot,
Awkwardness would be right behind her.

Laura's normally quiet,
It's occasional when she speaks,
If she speaks it would last around ten minutes,
Then hibernation is where she'll go!
But anywhere she sets foot,
Awkwardness would be right behind her.

Hasina is the set-up,
The one who always speaks,
She cannot keep her mouth shut,
Not even for a peep.
But anywhere she sets foot,
Awkwardness would be right behind her.

Precious, she's the troublemaker,
Don't let the name fool you,
One way or another
She'll be in an argument before you can say
Onomatopoeia! But she is nice . . .
But anywhere she sets foot,
Awkwardness would be right behind her.

Adora's straight up crazy,
No one can put out her flame,
She always gets the blame,
Each day with her is never the same,
But anywhere she sets foot,
But awkwardness will be right behind her.

Now do you see what I mean?
Yeah . . . no.
I don't get it still.
You just described six girls.
Go back, read the title,
And look at the italic letters . . .
Oh yeah . . .
Nausea!

Andrea Etim (11)
St Benedict's Catholic College, Colchester

 # Self Destruction

Love is unavoidable
Love is inevitable
It's everywhere you go
Our world is violent, our world is cruel
But love is still there - you can feel it in the air
She makes me feel oblivious to everything around me
She makes everything disappear
I get injected with the thought of her
I get injected with her one-of-a-kind beauty
For loving her is the most exquisite form of self-destruction.

Luigi Sombilon (13)
St Benedict's Catholic College, Colchester

Society's Rules

Society's rules,
All rule you,
So let's face it,
You can't win either way,
And everyone's trying to be a part of,
The kids who fit in,
If I do great at school,
I'm a teacher's pet,
If I fail like others,
I'm then 'cool',
If I use bad language
I'm a wannabe,
If I speak well,
I'm a loser,
If I don't make comments on others,
I'm a goodie-two-shoes,
If I do make a comment,
I'm a bully,
If you're too short,
You're a midget,
If I'm too tall,
I'm a giant,
If I don't have:
Facebook,
Instagram,
Twitter,
I'm not connected,
If I don't wear fashionable clothes,
I don't look right,
If I do wear fashionable clothes,
They don't suit me,
If I don't take things like,
Alcohol,
Drugs,
Cigarettes,
I'm a coward,
But at least I have respect for myself,
Because society doesn't.

Do I care?
No.
Should you?
Definitely not!

Mia Andrea Patterson (11)
St Benedict's Catholic College, Colchester

 **Poetopia**

Me.
A teen as they say.
But what really is a teen?
Is it a stroppy, moody teen,
Is it a helpful, caring teen,
Or is it a normal teen?
No one knows.
We say normal,
But what is normal?
Is it acting normal?
Is it being normal
Or is it pretending to be normal
When you're just secretly crazy?
But then we ask ourselves,
What is crazy?
And what kind of crazy?
Mental crazy?
Weird crazy?
Normal crazy
Or just plain crazy?
A teen
Confused
Like one in a thousand fish in the sea
Confused
As confused as a duck who forgot
How to swim,
Me, a confused teen, but still like dust,
I rise.

Kristen Thomas (13)
St Benedict's Catholic College, Colchester

◯ Dream On

Her hair was smooth and her cheeks were red,
But her eyes were cold and filled with dread,
Her dress was dark but her frills were white,
Her bonnet was black, her ribbon tied tight.
Along her young forehead ran a deep furrow,
Shadowing long-lost years of pain and sorrow.

The moon's ghostly face shyly entered the night.
Instantly, clouds ambushed it and obscured its light.
Now that her world was enveloped in darkness,
Now that it was cold, lonely and starless.
She lay down beneath a small sycamore tree.
A lingering life with a miserable end was all she could foresee.

Numb and forlorn, she let out a deep sigh,
Bitter tears tickled her cheeks as she started to cry.
Like dewdrops, they were sprinkled on blades of grass.
The night was old when she closed her eyes at last:
Her forehead softened, once more she was a child,
Dimples appeared in her cheeks as she softly smiled.

She dreamt of happiness and her young tender years,
Forgetting all her lingering worries and fears.
Outside of her blissful, heavenly dream,
The rains started to hiss and the winds, to scream.
A pallid hue spread across her skin,
Her cheeks looked drawn, and her hands so thin.
The dark quivered, as it shrieked and let out a wail.
The glorious morning had come; radiant and pale,
But she slept on beautiful but forsaken,
As she laid there still; never to awaken.

Inge-Maria Christine Botha (11)
St Benedict's Catholic College, Colchester

Why Should You Slay An Animal?

Why should you slay an animal
When you could let it stay alive?
Everybody deserves to survive.
So I never eat meat,
I find some other treat.
Why stick a hen in a cage and make it cry?
Why eat a sausage and let a cow die?
Do you still think: meat is right?
Despite the fact a cow can live to twenty-five
If the farmer allowed it to survive
But when it's three, it is sent to the shop.

Why not let a poor rabbit hop?
Instead of getting a gun.
And enjoy the fun of caring and sharing
And being kind to others?

Treat pigs like your sisters and brothers.
Why not have them as pets,
And why not give tofu and soya a try?

Don't see a chicken as lunch, don't see a cow as beef.
Pigs are not pork. No! Crab salads are not cool.

Hot dogs and hog roast are not 'hot, man'
Sizzling sausages are sick
But not as in cool
I mean as in *cruel*
You can instead eat gruel!

Jack Frampton (11)
St Benedict's Catholic College, Colchester

They're Going To Get Me

Shh! Come quick!
I'm scared, lonely and desperate.
I can run, but I can't hide,
I'm just a guiptian child.
They're going to get me,
The gobblers are going to get me.

Some people say they eat you!
Others say they kill you!
Some people say they're monsters,
And others say they're normal people.
But I still cannot escape it.
They're going to get me,
The gobblers are going to get me!

All the other kids joke about it,
Play about it, laugh about it.
The few like me, we shake about it,
Quake about it, we know it's not a game.
I know it, I know it, I know it!
They're going to get me,
The gobblers are going to get me.

I'm in a van,
Headed north, the lady with a golden monkey.
She seemed sweet but she is sour.
I miss my mum, I miss my dad,
They've got me,
The gobblers have got me.

Esme Bishop (12)
St Benedict's Catholic College, Colchester

 # Why?

We walk
And walk
And walk and walk
Until . . . the end
Of life, love, hate, anger
Just nothing, we stop.
And stare at nothing
Blackness, darkness, nothingness
We are consumed by this darkness
With no escape.

I will sometimes stop
And stare into a mirror
And wonder
Why am I here? Why do I exist?
Why do I get to live and so many others die
And fade, fade out of people's memories?

I wonder if we can escape
Just grab our bags and go
Leave everything and escape
Escape death, escape emotion, escape life
But I am a small pawn in a big game of chess
All I may hope for is a place
Where no worries exist but
I still come to the dark pit of death
Because truly
I will never escape.

Nathan Linscott (13)
St Benedict's Catholic College, Colchester

Gymnastics

Floor routines and rings,
Along with parallel bars,
The strength that is required,
Is well beyond what's ours!

You flip and you roll,
With grace you move,
Only an incredible gymnast,
Has nothing to improve.

Three days a week,
I tumble and fall,
Every single injury,
Was worth it all!

Late every night,
You're still in the gym,
Perfecting your skills,
So you can win!

The competition lasts for moments,
Though the training has taken years,
It wasn't the winning alone that was,
Worth the work and the tears.

Gymnastics alone
Is what gets you through,
Because it's not just a sport,
It's my life!

Olivia Farry (11)
St Benedict's Catholic College, Colchester

The World Surrounding Us

The world surrounding us
People do as they do
May all seem so boring to you
But no one sees what I see
The world surrounding us
The little things that go unnoticed
Is not something to go past.
The texture a pencil makes on paper
Or even the patterns of water vapour.
The millions of specks of dust floating in air
That no one sees but is still there.
The ordinary things that we may dread
Like weather with changes that are unsaid.
But like all things, there is beauty inside
Which as bad things happen, with time you leave aside.
Autumn with its brown leaves falling from trees
And in these months of cold weather you feel a breeze.
Spring with its warmer weather and blooming things,
After the cold winter, beauty it brings.
Summer for fun and hot weather too,
Must be enjoyed to the max and partied through and through.
So what I want to say is this
You should look at the day for what it is
As there will never be one quite the same.
Why are we so blind to see,
The wonderful things that this world could be?

Maria Houlden (13)
St Benedict's Catholic College, Colchester

Something To Believe In

War and hatred all need to go,
But how to do this, I don't know.
Some of us just don't care,
So I give them a hateful glare.
When I tell them, they just grin,
What they need is something to believe in.

Screams and shouts are all I hear,
I just wish they'd disappear.
Why can't we all just get along,
And not do what we know is wrong.
How I wish I could take them for a spin,
They need something to believe in.

Believe in love, believe in power,
Shout it from the tallest tower.
Any little thing will do,
As long as you stay true to you.
Now it is starting to begin,
They are finding what to believe in.

Who knows what you could do,
When you have an independent view.
Make a speech, take a bow,
Do anything, it's your world now.
Today is the day of your big win,
They have found something to believe in.

Katie Owens-Davies (11)
St Benedict's Catholic College, Colchester

Guitar - Haiku

Cool new set of strings
Now I can play anything,
Oops! Snapped my A string.

Kezi Harris (13)
St Benedict's Catholic College, Colchester

A Sandy Smooth Beach

The ocean tide began to stroll in,
As did a pitch-black sight,
The warm night air rushing through my hair,
As I sat on a sandy smooth beach,
Oh boy,
How I wish to fall asleep in this very place,
But no, for I have to go back home,
To meet my bed through this journey of the night.

I sit at the seashore watching the starry sky,
My imagination drifting far and wide,
My feet damp from the cold and frothy sea,
My eyes almost closed but yet they still see,
Oh boy,
How I wish to fall asleep in this very place,
But no, for I have to go back home,
To meet my bed through this journey of the night.

As I walk across this beach,
Memories flood my mind,
Of those old days,
In which the sun used to beam upon one's head,
Oh boy,
How I wish to fall asleep in this very place,
But no, for I have to go back home,
To meet my bed through this journey of the night.

Freya Josephine Rose Richardson (11)
St Benedict's Catholic College, Colchester

My Poem

Down in the deep deep of me,
A light appears,
Illuminated music sings,
Iridescent dresses shimmer,
Emerald, sapphire, ruby,
Leaping up, pointing toes
Majestically enchanted across the stage,
Three a line beneath the lights,
Skin tone soft,
Explosion of noise,
Tap, bang, clipping, clapping,
Cacophony of sound,
Three minutes, tick-tock, tick-tock,
Floating high, transcendent,
Symphony of dances,
Reel,
Slip jig,
Heavy,
Hornpipe,
Flying by time,
Results waiting,
Tummy butterfly nervous, patient,
Winners' radiant, glowing luminous,
Trophies held smiling.

Amaia D'Souza (11)
St Benedict's Catholic College, Colchester

 # No Idea . . .

I don't know what I'm meant to do,
I've tried and tried to think this through!

My brain is empty on what to write,
I've thought and thought with all my might.

They say you think best without your focus,
But my ideas aren't magic like hocus-pocus!

Racking my brain is not an easy task,
Why can't you get poems if you just ask?

Such stupid things, they do distract,
Like on my keyboard, is the cat.

Oh no, my dad is here,
At last night's party, he had too much beer!

I'm at my computer trying to type,
I need ideas fresh and ripe.

The TV is driving me crazy,
As for me completing this poem, that looks hazy.

I need to get this thing done,
So I can game and have some fun!

When you listen, don't boo and hiss,
But thinking of it, I'm writing this!

Peter Conway (12)
St Benedict's Catholic College, Colchester

War: The Everlasting Fear

War
An everlasting shadow of doom
Always going
Neither side retreating
Fear blanket covering, sucking the light from life

War
Guns drawn
Blood shed
Orphans, widowers
And motherless children
Less meaning nothing

War
Destroying old alliances
That were once strong
Brother turned on brother
Until nothing is left

War
Unmerciful
In despair
Fear, hate
When will it end?

Shannon Payne (11)
St Benedict's Catholic College, Colchester

Free

Drowning in their words deeper and deeper
Locked in her mind nobody hears her
Just a lost soul adrift in the sea
When all she wants is to be free
Free from life, free from worry
And for them to say they're sorry.

Georgia Spicer-Manning (13)
St Benedict's Catholic College, Colchester

 # Society

Welcome to society
We hope you enjoy your stay
And feel free to be yourself
As long as it's in the right way
Make sure you love your body
Not too much or we'll tear you down
We'll bully you for smiling
And then wonder why you frown
We'll tell you that you're worthless
That you shouldn't make a sound
And then cry with all the others
As you're buried in the ground
You can fall in love with anyone
As long as it's who we choose
And we'll let you have your opinions
But please shape them to our views
Welcome to society
We promise that we won't deceive
And one more rule now that you're here
There's no way you can leave.

Haydn Milkins (12)
St Benedict's Catholic College, Colchester

 # Friends

Some friends help you when you fall,
Others come only when you call.
Most leave you without a trace,
Some share their strawberry lace.
Others send a shiver down your spine
But, if you're lucky you'll have friends
Just as good as mine!

Ciara Lucy Rowe (12)
St Benedict's Catholic College, Colchester

Ollie The Dog

There once was a dog called Ollie,
Who was always rather jolly,
Then one day, in the middle of May,
He went out for a play,
He played for hours in the flowers,
And discovered he had super powers,
He flew off into the night,
But gave his neighbours a fright,
As he flew through the air,
He gave the public a terrible scare,
He finished his flight and came to land,
Then he met a famous pop band,
They played him a song which he loved,
But then he spotted a murder glove,
He took the glove and tested its DNA
Then the murderer was going to pay,
They found the man, which made him happy,
Then home he went to eat his Chappy,
He got a treat which was a lolly,
That turned him back to normal Ollie.

Josh Winfield (12)
St Benedict's Catholic College, Colchester

Life's Puzzle

Life has the structure of a book,
It's a series of events, forever changing and adapting,
Exactly like a puzzle,
Eventually all the pieces will fit together,
This creates a story,
After a while you have to turn the page,
Which creates a whole new life.

Elkan Baggott (11)
St Benedict's Catholic College, Colchester

 # Spring Breeze

A cascade of colour pops into the bitter
night air as the last bare leaf
surrenders to the white sheet of snow

An array of freshly cut grass bolted into action
as they swayed from side to side.
Insignificant pecks of luscious green exploded
up behind the trees
and danced joyfully, launching an
array of dandelions and blossoms.

The snow abandoned itself.
The darkened clouds took off, scared.
The trees sank to the ground
jumping up again filled with coral blossoms.
The snow vanished to form a
prodigious puddle as time revealed a sunny sky

It was the best of times; it was the worst of times,
actually it was springtime as the warmth of a spring day
spread across the garden in one joyous moment.

Sophie Pereira (11)
St Benedict's Catholic College, Colchester

 # Parents

Parents, they drive you everywhere.
Parents, all they do is care.
Whether it's pink, green or blue they know what's right for you.
They love you, feed you and treat you every day.
You may not know it but they're there for you every step of the way.
They might say they hate you and they might say they don't care.
But you really need to remember you'll always be their little Care Bear.
Parents make money mostly for you.
Just to buy you everything new.

Anton Alvrarez (12)
St Benedict's Catholic College, Colchester

In The Mountains

Skiing down the mountain,
Oh what fun!
Like a river cascading,
In the glowing sun.
The snow shines bright,
Oh what a sight!

Charging down at speed,
Is all I need.
Although it's chilly,
And I may look silly,
In my granny's knitted hat,
But I love my nan, so that's that.

The frost might bite,
The slopes may be steep.
The winds might squeal.
And the clouds might weep.
But the great mountain peak,
Is where I find the joy I seek.

Bandi Cserep (11)
St Benedict's Catholic College, Colchester

 # Winter

Snowflakes slowly drifting down
Falling to the ground
Ice-cold winds as fast as a cheetah
Making your heart pound
Blizzards swirling like a hurricane
A blanket of snow forming, as white as a cloud
Sitting by the warm blazing fire
Snowmen standing still and silent
Fields and houses covered in white
Winter is here!

Annabel Harper (11)
St Benedict's Catholic College, Colchester

Corrupted

This world is filled with corrupted people,
This world is filled with hate.
I wish this world could be different,
I wish there was nothing to care about.
I want to leave this place,
I want to smile again.
Violence, corruption and other bad things too,
They're all the things happening all around you!
I'm sick of being stuck in this dark place,
I'm sick of having this frown on my face.

All we do is judge,
Why can't we just eat some fudge?
Who cares about the weight we're gaining?
We were all made for a reason; for fighting.
When I'm eating all day,
I already know what you'll say: 'You're fat!'
But I don't care,
I'm leaving this place.

Molly Lear (13)
St Benedict's Catholic College, Colchester

Sea Of Wonders

Tick-tock, tick-tock,
The clock hit the hour,
Drip-drop, drip-drop,
The sea of tears hit the wall.

Tick-tock, tick-tock,
How long will it take?
Oh, how long?
How long till the sea reaches me?
Bringing all the wonders of joy and sadness?
Oh, how long?

Gabriela Witkowska (12)
St Benedict's Catholic College, Colchester

Football!

Football is my life,
It is my love,
My passion,
Everything I can imagine.

Messi, Ronaldo and Neymar.
How do they become the inspirations
That they are?

Ibrahimovic, Ronaldo and Messi,
They're all good kickers,
But personally I prefer the skillers.

My favourites are Hazard, Neymar and Messi,
They're all super pacey.
I really like Hazard but he's not really for me.

Messi is fast, intelligent
And a really good dribbler.
But none of them stand out as much as Neymar.

Matthew Birch (11)
St Benedict's Catholic College, Colchester

 # Just Me

Just me.
Just me alone in a room,
Full of all the memories from my past,
Stuck in time, not knowing who I will be,
Not knowing what will happen next,
Not knowing who I will meet.
I am confused,
Stuck in my mind,
Worrying, thinking, scared,
About my next step.
What will be next?

Ruby Buijs (12)
St Benedict's Catholic College, Colchester

Beautiful Snow

Oh beautiful snow
Everyone knows
It's the time of year
To spread goodness and cheer.

When the snowflake hits the ground
It will never ever make a sound
All the children smile
They know it only happens once in a while.

The snow is as white as the clouds
You always hear the kids shout out loud
Every child wearing a hat, scarf and gloves
Showing all forms of kindness and love.

It's always freezing cold
Most kids are told
Keep warm and don't hurt yourselves
Santa is coming with his little elves.

Cieran Montgomery (11)
St Benedict's Catholic College, Colchester

18

Since I was 18,
You've made me cry,
You've made me laugh,
You've made me smile,
You've made me understand who I am on the inside.

Today is our 10-year anniversary,
I don't want to lose you,
Take me in your arms,
I don't need you to buy me flowers,
I don't need your hugs,
I just want to know you love me.

Kelsey Davis (11)
St Benedict's Catholic College, Colchester

Only Present Now

I loved the past,
It went so fast,
It all happened in a blast,
I loved the past!

Now I am surviving on the scraps,
Unfortunately I have no maps,
Exploring through the gaps,
I need some maps!

Now it's all about pain,
Which is totally lame,
Bandits taking over the fame,
Which is totally lame!

I lost it all,
When civilisation began to fall,
It happened when I was in a mall,
I lost it all!

Jeremy Ozkaya-Simms (11)
St Benedict's Catholic College, Colchester

Where We Went Wrong

I shout, you leave
You leave, I beg you to stay
You get angry, I get upset
There's no way to explain the pain
We stopped checking for monsters under our bed
When we realised they were inside us
You take me through a guilt trip
Wondering where we went wrong
I count my tears while you're on
Your knees asking me to love you
The way I did.

Ncobile Phadi
St Benedict's Catholic College, Colchester

Parents

You clean my clothes
You make me dinner.
You're not losers
You're winners.

What you do for me
I really can't explain.
And how do you put up with me
Every . . . single . . . day?

I know I'm a pain
So do you.
Remember, remember, remember
I'm always here for you.

You help me when I'm down
You help me when I'm stuck.
Is there anything you can't do?
Except saying I love you.

Jay Alvarez
St Benedict's Catholic College, Colchester

Turkey

We party together
We feast together
Your crunchy skin
Protects what's in
You can fry
You roast
You poach
You steam
You boil
You're a part of life
Which dies when cut with a knife.

William Roper (11)
St Benedict's Catholic College, Colchester

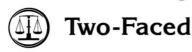

Two-Faced

I got a selection of faces
Each day I pick out one
As I decide who I will be
What will show everyone.

Out into the world I go
With whichever one I choose
Thinking that no one will notice
Only myself do I fool.

I pose one way to many
Turn around and show something different
Forgetting that others are watching
They pick it up in an instant.

Before I know what has happened
My faces get all out of place
Soon I'll find I'm wearing more than one
I have become two-faced.

Julian Olivagi (11)
St Benedict's Catholic College, Colchester

My Dad Is The Best
In The World

My dad is the best in the world.
He loves me with all his heart.
He has given me strength,
He has given me courage
But most of all
He has given me love.
I am his little helper, his little man, his little pride.
But no one can deny that,
I am proud to be his little man.

Tom Brown (12)
St Benedict's Catholic College, Colchester

⭕ Untitled

I walk through the sandy rocks
And see the boat-filled docks;
Walking slowly down the stairs
Surrounded by the people's prayers.

The horizon is a flaming red;
A seascape made by those who bled.

I run away quickly, through sharp stones
Not caring as they pierce my bones;
One mistake and my life is gone,
But the monster I will con -
I will set a trap, just for him
To tear that beast, limb from limb.

Burning red eyes nearing the trap,
All his energy I will sap -
One last step and he'll be dead;
The monster, at last, will be shred.

Jackie Chen (11)
St Benedict's Catholic College, Colchester

🕊 Why Me?

Standing there with blood trickling from his hands, wondering, *why me?*
How can someone so precious to him push him to do such a thing?

As a cold breeze ran across his face
He watched as the life he took away lay there helpless and pale
He couldn't believe this was happening to him.

He dragged the lifeless body and buried it in the deep, dark pit
And covered the evidence up.

He ran home with painful fear running through his blood
And his heart pounding like mad, wondering, *why me?*

Michelle Ukane (13)
St Benedict's Catholic College, Colchester

Pizza Night

I remember the joy I felt when I saw
It was pizza night,
The delectable slice of heaven,
It was a beautiful sight.

As I finished the last pepperoni,
And realised I was done,
I reached out for another slice,
And found out the pizza was gone!

The only thing left was crumbs,
On the empty-looking plate,
A tear rolled down my cheek,
I felt horribly dismayed.

I was utterly devastated,
But I wiped my tears away,
The realisation dawned on me,
Tomorrow was chip day!

Maddie Barrell (11)
St Benedict's Catholic College, Colchester

My Only Friend

I love you so much
And I miss your warm touch.
Your eyes are so bright,
They fill me with delight.
Your face, like gold,
And you never grow old.
But throughout the years
You helped me conquer my fears,
With arms open wide,
You've always been by my side.

Adora Kadri (11)
St Benedict's Catholic College, Colchester

✚ My Cat

My companion in my house is my cat.
She's black and sleek but is quite fat.
Although she lounges round all day,
she's always ready to come and play.
When I get home from school
she's always ready to play the fool,
trying to climb on this and that,
when resting she loves a stroke and pat.

When I came home from school one day,
she was a little too ready to play.
As she came bouncing on all fours
she smashed her head against the door,
then lay bemused upon the floor.
Rather surprised, she opened her eyes.
I was relieved to see she was fine,
I would be lost without this cat of mine.

Jared Chelski (11)
St Benedict's Catholic College, Colchester

⚖ Stop

They fight, not knowing it hurts inside.
They know their consequences, they don't care.
I feel like I'm the older one.
The adult, the one who should know best.
But I'm nobody, just a victim in a game,
A game I didn't want to play.
I just want the world to stop.
Being so rough with each other,
I want normality,
I want to be the person I was before.
I want everything to freeze,
To stop.

Anjola Akinboh (11)
St Benedict's Catholic College, Colchester

Lost Thoughts And Dreams

Hopes and dreams lost,
Gone to the back of my mind.
Forever lost.

Thoughts of becoming greater, better.
All gone. All washed away with my tears. RIP.
Forever lost.

Memories distraught,
As one daydream to be noticed.
Forever lost.

One day all will be
Unlocked and I will
Search for more
Dreams I
Have
Lost.

Nuala Brosnan Wren
St Benedict's Catholic College, Colchester

Paradise!

Paradise
Where sand and sea sparkle and palm trees sway
The beach as bright as the sun
The air is filled with the sound of crashing waves
The ocean is moving to the rhythm of crying gulls
With fresh coconut milk in my hand
The beaming rays of the sun heating up my skin
Swimming in the bright blue sea
Surrounded by a rainbow of fish
I feel a brush on my leg
A turtle gliding by
This is my paradise.

Johnny Albert McKew (12)
St Benedict's Catholic College, Colchester

 # Regrets

Some friends will take you down,
Like a picture off the wall.
Rarely some will catch you,
Even when you fall.

When you thought they were your friend,
They can always let you down.
Some friends are valuable,
But others aren't worth a pound.

Friend or foe, do we ever really know?
One day we're best buddies
The next we're going toe-to-toe!

I don't have many friends,
I could count them on my hand.
Not for the want of trying,
But life never goes as planned . . .

Chloe Oakley (11)
St Benedict's Catholic College, Colchester

 # Friendship

Friendship is like caring
And also like sharing.

Friendship is not arguing
Or getting into fights.

Friendship is being kind to others
And not thinking about yourself.

Friendship is talking
When people are alone.

Friendship is what God created
And makes us all happy.

Heidi Marie Walklett (12)
St Benedict's Catholic College, Colchester

 # Love

Love is like a rose,
But watch out for the thorns.
Love is like a patch of black ice,
You don't see it until you fall.
Love is like a hedgehog,
If you handle it right you won't get hurt.
Love is a maths equation,
It takes two to work it out.
Love is like an eel,
It can slip away easily.
Love is like a can of Coke,
If you shake it too much, it will fizz over.
Love is like laughter,
Addictive and unstoppable.
Love is like a patch of stingy nettles,
If you fall in it will hurt.

Danielle Martin
St Benedict's Catholic College, Colchester

 # Mother Nature

The beautiful hills
Revealing themselves to the sunset
Lay in awe
Of the overwhelming orangey red sky

The quiescent river
Cascading down the steep mountain
Gushing through the crevices
Falls into the unknown abyss

The lush green meadow
Flooded with summer daisies
Rises up into
The bright blue sky.

Max Chilver (11)
St Benedict's Catholic College, Colchester

The Monster

As the very patient mess-maker stands with his family,
He waits impassively, desiring to be used.
At last his moment finally arrives; he beckons to be fed,
His owner hears his calling he takes him to start work.
Now the monster is hungry,
He wants to start eating his large amounts of food.
He opens his jaw widely he listens and obeys,
He hungrily devours and separates his food.
The glistening white paper,
Is sliced into shreds,
The monster - super hungry.
Will he ever stop?
Now the owner's satisfied,
He puts him with his family.
The very patient mess-maker says,
'My circle re-begins.'

Chenile Sulley (11)
St Benedict's Catholic College, Colchester

Friendship

Side by side,
Or miles apart,
Friends are always,
Close at heart.

Friends are loving,
Friends will always share,
Friends will lend a helping hand,
When we are in despair.

So if you have friends like mine,
Who are always there for me,
If all it seems to do is rain,
They'll be there to set you free.

Annie Salthouse (11)
St Benedict's Catholic College, Colchester

Untitled

The rage, it consumes me
Keeping me awake
The memories burn strongly
The relentless attacks
From the bullies, why won't they stop?

All the punches, all the kicks,
All the name-calling, I can't let it get to me
I won't let it get to me
But it's just too hard, almost impossible
I have to do something, anything at all
The problem is . . . I don't know what.

Too hard to forgive, too hard to forget
Nothing I can do except let it carry on.
No one would help me, they wouldn't understand
This pain can't last, I don't want it to.

Zachary Askham (11)
St Benedict's Catholic College, Colchester

Death And New Life

Death
Surrounds me like a cloud
I can't run away from this cloud
I'm tied by a single thread
Family fall into the void
I'm stuck, waiting.
Deep down
Somewhere
A ray of light that makes grey clouds
White
And full of pure spirit and happiness
I just have to dig deep
And release the positive energy below.

Zylo Green (11)
St Benedict's Catholic College, Colchester

Pain And Regret

If I could turn back time, I would.
Change everything that happened, if I could.
But there's no such thing as time machines
So I've got to live with what I've done.
What I've done.
What I've done.

What have I done?

It won't change, not ever.
Even if I beg her.
My regret feels like the Devil has burned my heart.
But I can't do this any longer
'Cause the pain is getting stronger.
But I know you're sure,
And before you close this door.
I love you to infinity.

Natalie Madziyire (11)
St Benedict's Catholic College, Colchester

The Life Of A G

Rhyme skills is what I've got,
These rhymes will make yours rot,
Powerful as the SWAT,
Like a taser at 1,000 watt,
Say guilty you are not,
At the perfect moment slot,
Gang up and dash the lot,
As you watch their blood snot,
For them the moment's hot,
Their life is due to be forgot,
As I lead them away from my gangster plot,
Thinking this cannot be,
As I begin to flee.

Jonathan Last (12)
St Benedict's Catholic College, Colchester

This Generation

Wi-Fi is their source of power, sometimes their only friend
That source of electricity, an app or text to send
Can brighten up their day or even make one smile
Unless of course they're a gamer, then they stay straight-faced for a while
Social media ruins their brains and affects their time for school
But will they listen? Course they won't, so in school they drool
From lack of sleep and countless nights and when they're on their phones all day
They won't regret it, not one bit because that's this generation's way
Expensive phones and gadgets, drones, invented for the lazy
But what are we to say when we use them too? It drives society crazy
Apps and texts consume their day and their social skills
If they go over their text limits it can add to their parents' bills
And if you relate to any of these things then you should know you're in danger
Of Wi-Fi addiction and social awkwardness, for you are a teenager.

Kay Reyes (14)
St Benedict's Catholic College, Colchester

Velcro Child

When I was young my mum used to call me Velcro Child,
If you touched my feet I'd just go wild.
I'd always wear pink and hide in a blink.
Everyone would call me Velcro Child.

When I'm an adult I'll teach at a school,
Or even be a lifeguard at a swimming pool.
Though I've got years left to wait,
I don't want to start thinking too late.

As I'm going into my teenage years,
I've got many fears.
Sometimes I just want to hide in a box,
And swallow the key to the padlock.

Alice Haigherty (11)
St Benedict's Catholic College, Colchester

When I Am Older

I wonder, I wonder when I am older what will I be?
I wouldn't be a footballer because I would score in my own net,
And I wouldn't be a builder
Because I would do something silly like the bricks I would forget.
I wouldn't be a painter
Because the paint pot would fall and get stuck on my head.
Oh dear, oh dear, I will have to do something else instead!
I wouldn't be an actor because I would get booed off the stage,
And I wouldn't be a writer because I would only write one page.
I wouldn't be a priest because I would get bored and fall asleep,
And I wouldn't be a farmer because I would fall in the poo heap!
Umm . . . let me see, maybe there is something right for me!
Give me a moment while I think what that could be . . .
Ah, now I know it!
When I am older I will be a poet!

Joshua Velaquez Blanks (11)
St Benedict's Catholic College, Colchester

 # Humour Is In Everything

Humour is in everything
You can find it in whatever you do

When you dance or when you sing
You can find humour in anything

When you walk or when you talk
You can find humour in anything

When you think life is hard
Humour is the best medicine

If you laugh or even chuckle
Humour will always be there
To help you through the struggle.

Isobel Dullage
St Benedict's Catholic College, Colchester

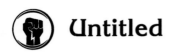

Untitled

I'm so angry,
Walls coming in,
I feel like it's the end of the world,
People just betraying me.
I can't take it anymore.
I'm so angry.
Help, hatred, it's coming back.
All the pain and words.
It's so frustrating, when I go to school.
People just bully me.
Call me names and pick on me.
I ask that this won't happen again.
Please take pity on me.
Mr/Mrs Bully, look I'm begging
On my knees.

Uzunma Osy-Orji (12)
St Benedict's Catholic College, Colchester

Thought

Tedious thoughts trickle
Into the brim of my thinking cap,
Cascading into my mind,
Suddenly flooded with ideas.
A brilliant rush,
Mind-blowing!
Going, going, gone . . .
My bubble burst.
Thoughts scattered around the classroom,
Back to square one.

Niamh Higgins (11)
St Benedict's Catholic College, Colchester

Friendship

I'd wait on you forever, and fly into some mush,
Because you and me together don't have to be pushed.
And even if you decide alone time's what you need
I will be here waiting like I'm held up on a lead,
You'll always have my shoulder for whatever's gone on
Because if you didn't I couldn't live on,
And if I got mad and then you yanked my sleeve,
We'd still be best buddies tied together like seaweed
And when we leave high school for more than just a week,
I know that you'll be with me in college with my saved seat
And the same in uni, handing me some sheets,
I'd do all this for you, whatever you need
Because that is friendship and without it where'd we be?
I know we'll stay together until we pass our lives on
Because we're best buddies and it's what we live on!

Maddie Himsworth (11)
St Benedict's Catholic College, Colchester

Untitled

Your design is spectacular,
Twelve inches, thick, tasty,
Cheap cost,
You fill my life with pleasure,
You make me feel up when I'm down,
You alone are worth my money,
Nothing else compares to you,
If only others could share my love,
For you, Subway.

John Lynch (13)
St Benedict's Catholic College, Colchester

My Poem

One lovely day I met a lovely dove
Right before I fell in love . . .

I met this lovely boy called Ryan
Who was really tryin'

We fell in love on a lovely day
With peaches on a tray . . .

This lovely dove came back with a letter
That made me feel much, much better . . .

It said, 'Will you marry me?
And let this love be . . . '

All these feelings I cannot fake,
But all this pressure I cannot take . . .

Precious Malone (11)
St Benedict's Catholic College, Colchester

Test Results

At that moment I opened the envelope,
I thought about what could be in store,
It might be war if I get a bad mark,
So I remember all the time I spent revising,
My score may be surprising,
For the right or the wrong,
It might just happen,
As I slowly open the envelope I've been dreading,
My mind went blank,
I really hoped I would get a good rank,
I opened it,
I couldn't believe my eyes,
I got a great level,
But did I beat my rival?

Ella Sandys (12)
St Benedict's Catholic College, Colchester

The Wrong Neighbours

A scream,
A shout.
A kick on the door,
A kick in the toe.
Bottles of booze, spilling down her throat.
A wasted five minutes,
Every five minutes.
Every F bomb sounds like a real bomb.
Starts at 8pm, ends 3am.
Sometimes all she wants is money.
Money wasted on getting wasted.
But she isn't a tramp.
She isn't a psycho.
She's my neighbour.

Jamie Baker (11)
St Benedict's Catholic College, Colchester

Rebuilding Your World . . .

When you are trying to rebuild your life . . .
When you have been so used to blocking people out
When you need that person to make it all go away
When you find you can't trust anyone ever again
All you see is black clouds and gloomy skies
You want to surrender to God
But that power that drove you
Through rehabilitation has kicked in again . . .
'Be free' my heart is telling me
But my mind is telling me . . .
No, continue the fight!
Make it alright!
Continue the journey
And make it all go away.

Ellie Giger (12)
St Benedict's Catholic College, Colchester

 Emotion

I don't know how I feel,
I don't know who I really am.
Most of the time I am depressed,
I am anonymous.
I don't know how I feel,
I don't know who I really am.
Most of the time I am sad,
I am anonymous.
Now I stand alone, left out,
Thinking and wondering who I really am.
Sad and depressed,
Unhappy or happy with life;
I feel . . .
Anonymous.

Charlotte Tully (11)
St Benedict's Catholic College, Colchester

 Sweet Dreams

Jelly beans and jelly babies
Lots of colour and different flavours.
Gummy bears chewy
And Creme Eggs gooey.
Strawberry laces dangling
And cola bottles tingling.
Small white mice
All naughty,
But nice!

Niamh Mary O'Neill (12)
St Benedict's Catholic College, Colchester

Too Painful

As my blood boils and my heart's dark with clouds and rain,
I keep a straight face and show no pain.
In my head everyone's watching the tears,
Laughing, as through my head go worries and fears.
It's all because of this one little mistake,
I can't deal with the laughter, now my own life I take.

Tom Reid (12)
St Benedict's Catholic College, Colchester

A Poem Of The French Journalist . . .

Everywhere I look,
Either people are screaming, crying or praying,
I know I'm different,
I will stand tall,
Not fall,
Not be judged,
I know the Muslim terrorists are judging free speech,
They are also trying to get leadership,
To show what's right,
But they're not,
Not all Muslims are like it,
Some are kind, caring people,
As I think this I feel a shooting pain,
And I'm no more,
I fall,
Still thinking that this is not right,
The light leaving me,
All I can feel. All I can feel . . . is sadness,
I'm no more.

Ellie-Marie Taylor (12)
Stewards Academy, Harlow

Dimmer Switch

Autumn.
Lantern-bright house sprawls on spotless lawn.
Trendy shoes click on tarmac
Bespoke suits rustle.
Doorbell.
Smiles - not too bright, mind you -
Like a finger on an imaginary dimmer switch
Going for the hug. Reeks of perfume.
Kiss her on the cheek?
Best not.

Slip through front door
Shoes off? No. We aren't five.
Pointless, even to think about it.
At least nothing was spoken aloud,
Yet she's half-looking
Like you said something
Don't make eye contact. Glance around
With false appreciation -
Spotless, gleaming, children locked upstairs
Along with the comfort and old-fashioned music.

Living room. What fresh hell is this?
Scattered pre-friends, post-acquaintances
Glances, smiles
- Dimmer switch on -
Cocktail dresses
Avoid the one with the tie like yours.
At last! Someone you know
But it's Julia. Her husband died.
Don't say a word.
Keep thoughts to yourself.

Smile! Shake hands. She's presented her cheek.
Quick peck, then take refuge
In your thoughts, then the patio ice bucket.
Damn.
It was bring-your-own-bottle.
- Look up now -

Someone's standing there
Forever excluded from the inner circle
For lack of a dimmer switch.
Was he born without one?
Thoughts to yourself, remember.
And eyes can betray as much as ten words
So be careful.

Though, come to think of it
They're probably working on a device
That posts thoughts to Facebook
Daydreams to Twitter
Digitally pinned to a flatscreen TV
Where all can see them
Like a meaningless collage of
Meaningless faces
And meaningless dimmer-switched
Smiles to flick on and off like the miles and miles
Of small-talk you prepared
When you have bought booze.
Turn around. Stride through.
Don't shake hands. If anything, stare
At the switchblades they surely clutch in their pockets.
Frowns, misdirected at walls
Anything to avoid your unfashionable bluntness.
Leave this house, quickly now.
Walk back home
To someone who won't need your dimmer switch.

Except you didn't do that.
You stood staring at ice in the bucket
Sipped your designer alcopop, stared at its surface
Which, oddly enough, must have mirrored your brain
As you tried not to look at the man in the corner
Even when, in a misguided attempt to make conversation, he
- Upstart that he was -
Asked where you're from.

Elliott Johnson (15)
Stewards Academy, Harlow

Sid

I saw a boy getting beaten today,
Pushed to the curb and smashed in the face,
All because of his race.

It was an even fight, I said leave them to it,
Then a big guy came along,
Must have been 6'3',
Kicked him in the ribs and left him in agony.

He started to shout and cry as they ran far away,
We told him that one day they'll pay,
They stole his phone and also his pride,
Leaving three broken ribs swelling inside.

We helped him up and called him an ambulance,
But his friends led him away, protecting his manly pride,
Only 18 years old on New Year's Eve,
Beaten black and blue just because he was walking down the street.

Racism stops here.

Amy Louise Minton (16)
Tendring Enterprise Studio School, Clacton-On-Sea

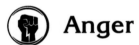

Anger

Anger is when a person goes mad at what the other person is doing to them . . .
Anger means being frustrated and anxious . . .
If you get angry you will go mad and do something bad.

So if you get a problem like someone starting on you
Go to the teacher rather than fixing it yourself
Always be good never be bad.

If you start a fight you will be beaten up very badly
And will end up in the hospital.

Daniel Sot
Voyager Academy, Peterborough

Monster

The monster's hair is as
Curly as string and ears green like Shrek's
He is huge, his mouth
Is like a cave but when he opens it you can see
His teeth like sharks'
He could kill you because
His muscles are
As big as rocks, his legs
Are as big as trees
If you find him you will need
To run because he is so
Scary, scarier than a ghost
He has a brother but
He looks like he is even
Scarier than his brother
They are as big as the sky
And his eyes are as blue as the sky
But there is a secret about
The monsters . . .
They are scared of frogs.

Osmantas Alisauskas
Voyager Academy, Peterborough

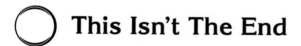

This Isn't The End

People fighting in the blood,
Running away from the sight
So I stumble across a hill
And falling down,
Rolling down
Finally hitting the ground
I take my last breath
Knowing this isn't the end . . .

Markuss Jansons
Voyager Academy, Peterborough

◯ The Room

I walk in complete darkness,
The wind brushes against my skin,
Birds cry in pain,
Floorboards squeak as I stumble, scared,
The place smells like death.
I brush my hand against the wall to find a sticky slime running down to the floor,
The creak of the door tells me it's time.

I curl up in a ball against the wall, terrified.
The lights start to flicker.
The birds stop and the room is silent,
Suddenly I can hear the scatter of the spiders
The room starts to get cold.
The wind is picking up but the smell is still there
The spiders are only inches away when I scream.

Now here I am,
In the same room on the same night,
Never allowed to leave.

Natalie Thomas
Voyager Academy, Peterborough

◯ Divergent

Scared and worried, determined to win
Don't want to have a test but that is all she has to do
Fight, fight, fight, and leave her family
She is divergent
Why does she have to be? Oh why, oh why?
Crying tears, needing help wondering why is she different to everyone else.

Natasha Ascott
Voyager Academy, Peterborough

◯ Hunger Games

Some other night,
A girl named Katniss,
Was chosen to run for her life.

Running in the forest,
Fire all around her,
Climbing on the tree
With her hurting leg.

The enemy was coming,
She was so scared,
Thinking what to do next.

Trying to escape,
Rue, a little girl, helped her,
The girl was kind and helpful too,
But another day someone threw
An arrow through her heart.
Now she was lying dead with flowers around her,
Katniss buried the little girl with honour and friendship as well.

Aleksandra Waligora
Voyager Academy, Peterborough

Monster

It was midnight, I was outside
I heard weird noises
I was scared
I turned around, I saw that ugly face
I ran away with a scream
I came back home
My mum didn't know what was going on
I told her everything
But she didn't believe me.

The next day I came back to that place
Where I saw the monster
But the monster wasn't there anymore
So I was looking for the monster
And finally I found him . . .

Julita Szalasny
Voyager Academy, Peterborough

Sophia

I ran through the woods
Zombies behind me
I clutched my doll tight
As I ran through the light
There was only one way to get away
The water . . .

So I jumped in without hesitation
As a zombie lunged at me
It knocked me into a zombie
It bit me on the left shoulder
As I screamed
My mum saw me like that
My dad pulled her away
I closed my eyes and turned . . .

Gabby Robinson
Voyager Academy, Peterborough

Love And Emotion . . .

K atniss is in distress, confused and lonely but has a little piece of love still left in her heart.

A ll she needs is love and confidence in herself to survive but with her sister gone, she begs for her back, but she is now lost with Peeta.

T ill now she has been waiting for her ticket home where she belongs, but now everything is changing and not going anywhere without a fight as most people have betrayed her or been excused for no reason.

N onetheless she is running, shooting for survival, getting used to trying to defeat the other districts.

I ntelligence, ups and downs, Katniss and Peeta survive together as a team. (With love and hope.)

S trength and victory all the better to succeed.

S afety for herself and Peeta caring for each other, no matter what.

Vesta Serzintaite (11)
Voyager Academy, Peterborough

Untitled

Always try your best
Always try your hardest
Always dress up smart
Never give up
Always be nice
Try to make friends
Never be mean
Don't try to attract attention
Never steal stuff that isn't yours
Never, never give up
Never surrender
If you do all of this, you will succeed.

Dominic Sell (11)
Voyager Academy, Peterborough

YOUNG WRITERS INFORMATION

We hope you have enjoyed reading this book – and that you will continue to in the coming years.

If you're a young writer who enjoys reading and creative writing, or the parent of an enthusiastic poet or story writer, do visit our website **www.youngwriters.co.uk**. Here you will find free competitions, workshops and games, as well as recommended reads, a poetry glossary and our blog.

If you would like to order further copies of this book, or any of our other titles, give us a call or visit **www.youngwriters.co.uk**.

Young Writers,
Remus House
Coltsfoot Drive,
Peterborough,
PE2 9BF

(01733) 890066 / 898110
info@youngwriters.co.uk